Come wind,
Come weather

Come wind, Come weather

A pilgrim's handbook of prayers and activities
for the length of Britain

Janet Lees

wild goose
publications

www.ionabooks.com

First published 2024 by
Wild Goose Publications
Suite 9, Fairfield
1048 Govan Road, Glasgow G51 4XS, Scotland
A division of Iona Community Trading CIC
Limited Company Reg. No. SC156678
www.ionabooks.com

ISBN 978-1-80432-339-7

Cover photo © Janet Lees

Overseas distribution
Australia: Willow Connection Pty Ltd, 1/13 Kell Mather Drive, Lennox Head NSW 2478
New Zealand: Pleroma, Higginson Street, Otane 4170, Central Hawkes Bay

Printed in the UK by Page Bros (Norwich) Ltd

Contents

Introduction

Pilgrimage is as old as the hills and as new as the sunrise, transcending every division of faith and belief. From the evidence of huge feasts at Durrington Walls near Stonehenge to the floral tributes left at roadsides and football grounds, it's clear pilgrimage is an important human activity. There's holy stuff all around us: in the landscape, in memory, in everyday life. Recognising that holiness and realigning ourselves so that we are focused on that engagement is key to the pilgrimage journey. We may claim any journey as a pilgrimage if that purpose resides in us. It depends on our intent.

Pilgrimage, an activity for anyone, has become more and more popular. More and more people have been looking for diverse ways to connect with the landscape and nature, and not just through formal pilgrimages. Build-your-own-pilgrimage is popular too and this book could help you with that. From routes and places, to habitats and species, there's a lot to engage with in these islands.

This book is also for the daily pilgrim for whom environmental concern is at the forefront of faith and life. It is for those who set out to travel sustainably every day, whether they go purposefully up the high street and see holiness all around or make a more dramatic journey to a well-known landmark. There are many types of pilgrimage guidebooks, but this one is more about the pilgrim opportunities on your doorstep the length of Britain. It took me 117 days to walk the length of Britain in 2019, a route of 1110 miles, but a journey of any length can be a pilgrimage.

I don't know when I first identified as a pilgrim but there are some salient moments in my memory, like my great-aunt's request to sing John Bunyan's hymn 'To be a pilgrim' after the death of my great-uncle. Words from that hymn form the title of this book. They had kept the fish shop together, and in my childhood there was no more holy place, as food and stories were shared and strangers and friends served there. All of these memories – and more – came back as I walked the End to End, the third member of my family to walk it. My husband Bob walked it in 2003; and my daughter Hannah walked it in 2012 when she was 18. I was 60 and recently retired when I set out on my own route from Land's End in April 2019, reaching John o'Groats four months later in August. During lockdown, when we were encouraged to take 'local exercise' every day, was a different kind of pilgrimage, as I remembered, revisited and retold the stories of many journeys.

It's now over four years since I walked the End to End. The memories are still strong and I think about it most days. It has affected the ways I walk, eat, pray and live in every way and influenced my thoughts about the climate crisis. That crisis is not a thing of the hypothetical future. It is happening now as species decline and habitats change. In some ways, writing a book about a walk seems self-indulgent. Yet it has made me even more aware of the landscape I walk through and the species I share it with. In 2023, on the way up the path to the Greenwich Observatory, part of the Greenwich Meridian Trail, I saw a lesser stag beetle lumbering along. It is one of the larger species of beetle in Britain, and this was the first time I'd seen one. Will it be the last? I hope not, and I also hope that sharing these thoughts, reflections and prayers will be a small contribution to urgently connecting us in new ways to people and beetles.

The first part of this book includes general pilgrimage things, many of which came from the experience of my End to End in 2019, which any pilgrim might use. The second part explores material for different ecological contexts found in Britain – from the sea to the mountains and everything in between.

I hope this book helps to equip you in your pilgrimage.

'Come wind, come weather,
there's no discouragement,
shall make us once relent,
our first avowed intent
to be a pilgrim.'

(John Bunyan, adapted)

Janet Lees

Note

This book uses the remembered Bible (RB), a personal version based on oral/aural rememberings and contextual experiences. You can find out more about my RB work in my publications at www.ionabooks.com:

Word of Mouth: Using the Remembered Bible for Building Community, Janet Lees

Tell Me the Stories of Jesus: A Companion to the Remembered Gospel, Janet Lees

I also try to write in inclusive language as much as possible. Thus I use the word 'kindom' to indicate a gender-inclusive, non-hierarchical community. May it include other species too.

Acknowledgements

Thanks to all those who have encouraged or supported my journeys, and especially to my husband Bob and my daughter Hannah, pilgrim companions.

Part One

To be a pilgrim

Getting started

Go out with joy, begin with peace:
there will be a cheerful way between the mountains and hills
and in the fields all the trees will applaud. (RB)

The basic requirement of pilgrimage is to have an intentional journey in mind. Long or short, distant or nearby, virtual or real, are not important, nor is the means of locomotion. You may get about any way you can. In some traditions it was considered important to use your knees, but it's fine not to. It's why you're going not what you are doing or how you're doing it that makes it a pilgrimage.

Some say there's a difference between tourism and pilgrimage but for me it's not so huge. Pilgrimage is for ordinary people, not the 'super holy'. 'Holiday' comes from 'holy day' and every holy day can be a holiday. The original tourists were pilgrims, buying stuff to weigh them down on their way to remind them that they had done the journey. We still do this, and many of the places that attract tourists today do so because they first attracted pilgrims, so there's no need to get bogged down with these distinctions.

Others might wonder if it is a religious activity, and I would say it depends on your thoughts about religion. Some find that a positive, others a negative, word. As one who straddles both church and non-church spaces, I believe it's fine to think of pilgrimage as what feeds you. You may want to reconnect with a place or space, retell a memory or story, count your blessings in the nature all around you, and for you that might be religious, or spiritual, or it might be a way of awakening to your full humanity. Pilgrimage can be an activity that unites us, both humans and non-human species.

Good practical preparation like maps, routes, prayers, clothing are important but should not limit our creativity on the way as the journey unfolds. As an aid to reflection afterwards, some might make a map of high and low points. If you have had a journey in mind for some time, then you may well have more resources ready than you think. Look inside you for your memories, stories and songs to call on as you go. I use my remembered Bible, the version that is in me, and you will find I refer to it in this book.

Pilgrims might like to start their journey with a few quiet moments of preparation. There are many ways of doing this and material in diverse traditions. Here are some of the ways of beginning a journey that I use and some other ideas and resources.

1. Getting to the line

At Land's End and John o'Groats there are lines marking the start/end points of the End to End. I always take a 'tigging' photo wherever I begin and end my journey if I can. Here's an activity that might be a sort of pilgrimage warm-up:

Before you begin, spend a few minutes thinking about how you will get along your pilgrimage. What body parts will you be using? Pilgrimage is an embodied thing: we take our body with us. Which parts of it will make the biggest contributions to getting you there? How important are limbs or lungs? We will each have capacities and impairments. We go with the bodies we have, not with perfect bodies, whatever those might be.

If you are in a small group, and it feels safe, maybe you can share some of your thoughts about your pilgrim body with one or two other pilgrims.

Today, I put my body on the line:
Let each cell begin the journey.
As I admire my form

and give thanks for this opportunity,
I praise God, Body Creator,
I reverence Christ, Body Inhabiter,
I welcome the Spirit, Body Transformer,
and in the power of the Holy Three,
I make this pilgrimage.

2. Prayers to get going with

Today, I travel in the power and presence of the Holy Three:
Creator around me,
Christ to accompany me,
Spirit to animate me.
In the power and presence of the Holy Three, I travel today.

If you start in the morning …

After darkness comes the morning.
The bright sun rises – Alleluia!
The Son comes amongst us – Alleluia!
More than 5000 creatures have already been fed.
Thank God!

If you intend to walk …

Holy One bless these feet,
bless these lungs and this heart,
as I breathe may I be reformed by your Spirit.

If you are using wheels …

Bless these wheels:
may they continue round and round
like the cosmic dance of the Holy Three,
Maker, Son and Spirit.

Other modes of travel are available … give thanks for the hooves that
clip clop – and give particular thanks for anyone giving you a piggyback.

3. Local saints

Every place has its local saints, or you may have favourite ones. You might like to remember them at the beginning of your walk.

For all the saints who honour small villages with their names
and faith stories:
We give thanks.

For all the saints who labour in all weathers to mend roads,
control floods or bring in the harvest:
We give thanks.

For all the saints who staff small shops, campsites and takeaways
feeding passers-by and locals:
We give thanks.

For all the saints, that they may duly rest from their labours.

4. Naming

You could begin with a naming activity. Naming is important. Remember how God invites Adam and Eve into the naming activity in the Garden of Eden. Places and species may have several names. A place may have a name given by former inhabitants or more recent ones. Creatures may have scientific or local names. When we were children, my brother and I used to make up names for things we didn't know the names of, like 'thistless thistle', the 'giant buttercup' ... A map can help with names of places and so can local stories. Whatever names you use, remember God is a Name-giver who values names.

5. The right to roam

Remember that the opportunity to walk freely is not universally available. In some countries it is restricted, and the right to roam was more limited in England before the Kinder Mass Trespass on 24th April, 1932. A recent Police and Crime Bill, 2021, limits the right to roam for Travellers and Roma people in England, who have long been marginalised and persecuted in this country and in Europe. It is estimated that between 200,000 and 500,000 Roma and Sinti people were murdered during the Holocaust, which the Romani refer to as 'the Devouring'. In the Global South walking is a necessity for many people: to get water, to take goods to market, to flee famine or persecution. It's not just the privileged leisure activity it is for me.

Forgive us our trespasses, we pray,
but some trespasses deserve remembering.
No walls, no borders:
may we, remembering your saints,
respond to the needs of the world
and its wandering people,
as they did of old,
making a home with the marginalised and rejected,
showing hospitality,
making God's call our priority.

6. Holy Week

Some people take pilgrimages at certain times of the year, for example during Holy Week. The traditional 'Journey to Jerusalem' is the foundation of the Christian idea of pilgrimage. If your journey is during Holy Week, you might want to use your remembered Bible to think about each day and reflect on Jesus' journey.

At the beginning of Holy Week

Creator, may your house be a sound and safe place to build community,
and a place that, like a launch pad, sets us on the journey,
keeping us in your orbit.
Companion Christ,
on the roads where crowds shout out, or alone on the silent path
may we keep company with you and be truly alive.
Holy Spirit, in this week of weeks,
animate our prayers and actions:
may we be wholly yours.

At the end of Holy Week

In the heat of the day,
when the sun burns its way across the sky,
and news comes in of more inhuman acts
and suffering beyond enduring,
it's hard to credit the notion
that a rock-rolling God
can move heaven and earth
to make all things new.
Through your life in us
may we be made new today.

7. Music on the way

When you're out there being a pilgrim, many things may help to keep you going. Some like a playlist they can tune into, but I like to make up my own songs, or recall old ones and embroider them with new meaning. Pilgrims have sung songs for generations. Many of the psalms began as pilgrim songs for those on their way to Jerusalem. One of the oldest songs in Britain, 'Clothing Dinogad', originated in Old Welsh, possibly in the seventh century, and may have been sung on the pilgrim road, perhaps from Cumbria to Anglesey.

I make up lots of songs or chants and some get sung more than once. Others fly away on the wind. This one is for St Martha the Dragon Slayer, whose Feast Day is 29th July:

Martha had many dragons to slay;
she would do it every day.
Walk right up and push them down:
She was the best dragon slayer in town.

Dragons come in many sizes
and wear a lot of different disguises.
They start off small and then they grow
and often have other dragons in tow.

Shoo, shoo, you dragons all be gone.
We will slay you one by one!
'Dragons!' we will all call out –
slay every dragon with a shout!

8. Counting

You might like to have some daily habits to help keep you on track.

Counting steps has become popular. Some places have been stepped on countless times. Tarr Steps in Exmoor, the site of an old clapper bridge, is one ancient crossing place made of stones. When the River Barle is in spate the stones have sometimes been swept away. Now each stone is numbered so that it can be retrieved after any flood and the bridge be reassembled, by number.

On Good Friday, of all days, we remember steps that count:
steps through Jerusalem's streets;
steps alone on a hard way with a heavy burden;
steps of another compelled to help, coming alongside;
steps taken knowing that death waits at the end of the road;
steps of those running away, steps of others standing nearby;
steps of a military guard;
steps of a crowd in narrow streets;
steps on stones, steps in dust;
steps to a criminal's death;
steps to the cross:
countless steps.

May we who step on the Way today
be sure to make every step count,
for the sake of Jesus.

You can count milestones or mileposts and some old routes have distinctive ones. Canals often have these and may also have numbered bridges that count up or down to your destination. The oldest milestones you can still

see in Britain are Roman ones, like the one in the churchyard of the Church
of the Holy Ghost, in Middleton, Cumbria.

Sticking up,
almost rubbed smooth,
witness to the passing legions,
I am reassured
by this simple stone:
AD, Anno Domini.

9. 'Thing of the day'

Since my husband, Bob, walked his End to End in 2003 it has become a
family ritual to look for a tree of the day. This tree can be any tree: it may
be old or young, deciduous or coniferous, standing alone or with others.
It is a tree that takes root in your imagination. It is a tree to celebrate. You
could photograph your tree of the day, or draw it, or make a rubbing of
the bark, or collect a leaf or fruit. You could give it a hug or stroke. All of
these things can connect you to your tree of the day.

But you may decide to notice other things too. You might like to photograph a plant or creature of the day from your encounters. This can lead
to a number of collectable hashtags, for example #fungusoftheweek. I also
like to photograph postboxes, especially old ones, but let your imagination
run with this one and see what you come up with. It could be a bird box
of the day, a signpost of the week …

Or you might like to pick up something small on your journey, perhaps
a pebble, a shell, a twig, a leaf … that for you embodies something of the
way. You might take it with you and perhaps leave it in some other place.

We are tactile people and having something to touch or hold can speak to us of our connections to the world around us.

Pebble in my palm,
dirt under my nail,
path under the sky:
may I go well.

10. Food for pilgrims

Edible stuff is important to pilgrims. You need to fuel your journey. I like to find local ice cream makers and sellers, as ice cream is a great substance for lifting the pilgrim's spirits. My highest tally is five ice creams in a day, but I've regularly made it to three. Local makers and sellers need your support. There's an ice cream trail in Scotland, and possibly in other places. Make the most of them.

You will also possibly find honesty boxes or stalls. Be generous with your honesty. Most sell food but some sell other things (T-shirts or candles for example). They may be in a phone box, a shed, on a wheelbarrow … They may combine both ice cream and honesty: a small freezer by the Shropshire Union Canal for example.

Look out for other foodstuffs that every pilgrim needs. In the British Isles the best of these is fish and chips. There are National Awards for fish and chip shops which you could research before you start. The Shap Chippy in Cumbria is one of the best, and likes to advertise its sustainable fish meals, but Kilmarnock, a small place in Scotland, also has a good one.

Depending on your season of walking you may find wild stuff to eat, or a fudge boat on the Trent and Mersey Canal to sample from. Don't eat wild stuff you aren't sure is safe: I'm thinking fungi and mushrooms here. Admire them but leave them be. Tasty wild raspberries, blackberries and bilberries can give a tangy sweet hit on the tongue just when your steps are flagging.

Pow!
May this mouthful give me power!

11. Meeting other travellers

This might be planned or random. Even so there are some places where you are more likely to meet fellow End to Enders. Land's End and John o'Groats, or at least in the first or last few miles, are the most obvious ones. The other is at the back road by the M6 at the Solway crossing, as this is the only way across the border in miles for non-motorway traffic and walkers. I was passed by a world-record contender Paralympic cyclist here in 2019 (she beat it).

When you meet other travellers

For the unexpected encounters:
the refreshment providers,
the craft shop proprietors,
the community volunteers,
the bell ringers and café servers,
for the lost, the bereaved and the lonely,
for families on days out,
for world record attempters,
and for all who offer support and encouragement,
this pilgrim is thankful.

Thanksgiving when meeting a friend

You entice me into relationship, into movement, into action.
We hold hands, glued together in faith and hope.
Your presence is a light.

12. An app

There are loads of walking apps. You can get the Ordnance Survey maps on apps but I still prefer paper maps. However, neither are particularly good in heavy rain, although you can get a plastic cover or map holder.

There are also wildlife apps that can help you to identify and record things you see. I have one to count butterflies, as this is something I enjoy doing while walking in spring and summer. As climate change advances and human activity threatens the habitats of many species, even the self-taught naturalist can make useful observations (counting adders for example) in a local area, or more widely, that help us to understand such changes.

Sitting in the sun or sliding along,
may my adding count.

God says, 'I know every bird in the mountains, and the insects in the
meadows are also mine.' (RB)

The drone of many bees hums in the background:
The countryside is alive with insects.
As I count butterflies one alights on my finger,
still for a few heartbeats,
before flying off towards the setting sun.
God grant a quiet night and a peaceful end.

With my phone, I photograph things that pop into my view and give a
nudge to a brain cell or two to make a connection between me and the
thing I'm photographing. This is itself a form of worship. I have noticed
what the Creator has made and I am grateful, glad and fired up.

13. Psalm snippets

Benedictines use psalms in their daily worship. I use psalm snippets: small
sections of remembered psalms suited to the day as it is revealed around me.
Use one or more of the following. You can tuck one into your memory and
walk with it through the day. These are just a few possible starting points:

One for weather-watching

God's loud voice breaks the cedars, even the cedars of Lebanon making the
mountains of Lebanon jump like calves. (RB)

It's not surprising that the Psalmist likened God's voice to thunder. It is a glorious sound. During storms trees are broken, groups of young cattle run up and down, clouds swirl overhead – it's quite a display. In the meadows the wild flowers continue to bloom. When the storm is over the rabbits emerge to see what all the fuss was about.

One for tasting

O taste and see … (RB)

I will trust the tasty all-seeing One.

I see a wild strawberry, small, rough – and red. One at a time on my tongue, their fruitiness bursts into my mouth. I will trust the tasty all-seeing One, maker of wild things and exploding tastes.

One for the way

Keep my feet from tripping up: may I walk with you on a life-giving way.
(RB)

The subtle grey light of a drizzly day,
the bright clear light of a blue sky day,
the soft light of the evening star:
each one gives us light and shows us a path.
You have brought me to a place where I may thrive.
You have shown me the grave and proved it empty.

One for being happy

People of all nations, every creature living, sing cheerfully to the Creator:
serve God with laughter, tell the endless story, come together and live
happily. (RB)

The hedges are alive with song, the sky wraps around the globe and holds
it all together. How I love God's endless story and how happily I tell it in
any company. (RB)

Other sections of your remembered Bible can provide snippets, for example
the Beatitudes.

Blessed are the walkers, the way-wanderers, the slow travellers:
they will experience the awe that comes with treading the earth gently.
(RB)

14. Grit

It's important to include plenty of grit. Travelling any day in any way can be demanding. It's not all sunny vistas. I often get stones in my boots or wet through to my underwear. I also get stuff running round in my head stirring up emotions and responses that I was hoping to handle with less effort.

It's great to see the glimpses of wildlife that lift my heart but it's also important to register the plastic pollution mounting up in the canal basin and the fly-tipping by the field gate.

These are some of the reasons why grit is important in the prayerful responses of any traveller.

Travellers have their anxious moments as well as their sad or angry ones. I count butterflies and other insects to lift my heart, but also to inform me of the way in which land use changes are contributing to the changes in species.

To go on an adventure is to engage in a daring or risky activity, so don't just pray prettily.

Grit in my shoe,
sweat between my breasts,
wet knickers,
wind blowing me sideways,
tears in my eyes,
worries in my head.
These are some of the little adventures in a big adventure.
Christ, have mercy.

To set out from shore
into unknown territory,

with limited resources,
unsure of a welcome,
swamped by anxiety,
overcome by uncertainty,
not a journey we'd embrace lightly.
Christ, have mercy.

May we who take the choice to travel in your name and company,
make the choice to support the weak and wandering,
the vulnerable, the unwelcome ones,
who, staggering to land, heads down, having left all behind,
show us a meaning to risk and jeopardy
that mirrors your Cross-Wise Way.
Christ, have mercy.

15. Challenges and disturbances

Pilgrimage is full of challenges: the terrain, the weather, the people and, for me, the dogs. If taking your dog on pilgrimage please consider other travellers. Even if you think your dog is a safe hound, this may not be or feel true for your companions. And consider where your dog might suddenly run to, depending on the season: ground-nesting birds are easily disturbed. Wherever you take your dog, please remember to clear up after it. Bags of dog poo adorning branches, or anywhere, are not a delightful addition to the pilgrim way.

If you intend to travel with others, plan things like whether you will travel together every day, and what you might do about any interpersonal difficulties that might arise.

Some pilgrims like to travel in silence or alone, others like to talk and share the path. Some like liturgical regularity with prayers at set times, maybe from a book. Others prefer spontaneity. If travelling with others, determine what is confidential to the group of travellers (in other words, 'what happens on pilgrimage, stays on pilgrimage'), or whether it's fine to retell stories or incidents to anyone else.

Together or apart,
accompanied or unaccompanied,
silent, still or thinking aloud,
respect the pilgrim way
and those who travel it.

16. Evening thoughts

At the end of your day's walking you may want some evening time for prayer and reflection. The phrase 'God grant a quiet night' is often used in evening prayers and so features here:

The birds fly home

The birds fly home to nest.
The bats leave their roost to make the most of the night.
For dark and light are both alike to the Creator.
Each creature has a place in the cosmos and in God's heart.
To each, God grant a quiet night.

Cooperation

Cooperation is crucial to community,
from the local to the global on our planet.
Cooperation runs a railway, a campsite or a pub.
As day turns to night and evening comes on,
may we be refreshed and made ready
for the cooperative activities of tomorrow.
To each, God grant a quiet night.

We come to you

Jesus said, 'Come to me all you who struggle' (RB)

We come to you, Jesus,
Living Way and true guide;
giving thanks for the satisfaction of daily progress,
the beauty of the trees and plants lining the path,
for places to rest and the refreshment.
We come to you, seeking the full life you promise:
God grant a quiet night.

17. Blessings

Blessings are a common aspect of many spiritual traditions. A blessing can be said at any time of day anywhere. Look around you and see in what ways you are blessed at that moment. What shows God's care for you and for all of creation?

May the waterway refresh you, may it lull you gently to rest.
May the trees shade you, providing a haven from wind and rain.
May the green plants entrance you, each one a feast for your senses.

May the birds entertain you and the world around you give you strength.
May you respond responsibly and with care in partnership
with people worldwide.
And may God grant all a quiet night and a peaceful end.

May the deer bound to greet you.
May the buzzard, watching, circle over you.
May the foxgloves trumpet your progress
and the waves applaud your arrival,
as you celebrate your daily progress
and travel on to the end of the road.

18. One of those days

What about those days when you can't make your pilgrimage?

Maybe there's more than one day – for any number of reasons.

What if bad weather, an unhelpful diary, an aching body and mind won't actually accommodate to pilgrimage for a day, or even more?

What if you're having 'one of those days'?

Can I make the pilgrimage from the bed to the bathroom?

Might Jacob's Ladder fill the space between here and the ground floor?

Might I open the window and, looking out under leaden skies, observe the route to the end of the yard, to the gate or to the balcony rail?

Heavy, that's how it feels to me when brain and body combine to root me to this spot. But I do have other pilgrim days to remember:

How tired I was halfway along the Great Glen, having already completed the West Highland Way – which in itself had been demanding. No wonder the little eco-café with its cake and friendly chickens seemed so appealing.

How battered I was on the top road near Janetstown, Caithness, with a hoolie blowing that had nearly knocked me over several times.

How misty it was at Gold Corner, as the drizzle enveloped me, soaking me thoroughly, and the cows were just like indistinct lumps in the landscape.

Sometimes there was a psalm that sprang into my mind of God watching endlessly from mountaintops, or cosseting me under wings, or mindful of me since I was in the womb.

Sometimes there was a ragged robin in flower, the thread-like pink strands blowing in the wind, or a ladybird tucked into a crevice.

One time there was an honesty deep freezer of ice cream and the hardest part was choosing which flavour to enjoy.

But mostly there were steps and one breath after another.

So on a stepless day, I still have that: one breath after another.

A blessing for the pilgrimage of the breath

May I/you breathe today, one breath after another.

May I/you breathe in the name of the Creator.
May I/you breathe in the company of the Son.
May I/you breathe in the promise of the Spirit.

In with the Three, may I/you breathe,
each breath touching each cell:
affirming, knowing …

Out may I/you breathe with the Three:
into air, into the world:
held, numbered …

And may that be my/your daily pilgrimage of breath:
The blessing of the Holy Three in each breath,
assuring me/you that I/you also count.

19. Remembering

When you have completed your pilgrimage you may want to remember your wanderings in a journal or scrapbook. I have kept scrapbooks since I was a child. They contain all sorts of stuff: tickets and timetables, pressed leaves and flowers, feathers and postcards … I don't usually put in lots of words, maybe a title or a few sentences. The stuff speaks for itself and evokes the memories and stories stored up in me. One that I made in Scotland when I was nine years old had a large prickly thistle on the front, a method of ensuring people didn't look inside uninvited. I still have it over fifty years later.

It can be helpful to have a notebook on the journey to help keep a record of your travels, or you may use an electronic device, or write a blog … As you travel you will gradually find the way that is right for you. It's good to look back on your journey. I often recall mine at particular times of the year and revisit significant days on different anniversaries. Journals and scrapbooks can be re-annotated to take account of new discoveries or fresh memories.

20. Commitment

The End to End was more than a walk. It was a time and opportunity to renew and refuel myself for the next part of my life as a person of faith. Each year I recall these times and such remembering provides an opportunity for recommitment in the company of the Travelling One, in what I've come to refer to as the Community of the Good Traveller.

End to End anniversary declaration

I inhabit a space made by the Creator,
lived in by the Son
and animated by the Spirit.
In that space around me and within me,
I commit myself anew
to the Community of the Good Traveller,
staying local where I can,
treading gently on the earth,
making each step count,
ready to salute the species around me
and celebrate our place in the universe.

21. A route

The kind of pilgrim you are will determine your route. Some of the variables will include the time available, your own access arrangements and abilities, the equipment you need, the weather … Standing at Land's End, I wasn't sure if I could actually walk all the way to John o'Groats but I had a route in mind. Some of it overlapped with previous routes taken by my husband and my daughter, some overlapped with old railways, canals and the ways of local saints. They would be strung together to create a green thread the length of Britain.

It's fine to have a short list of routes that you'd like to attempt some day. There are many more accessible routes for wheelchair-users, horse-riders, cyclists of all abilities and walkers, and these are being added to all the time. Do some research from books, websites and fellow pilgrims. Spend time collecting the things you will need. Work on your fitness. All of these things will contribute to a successful pilgrimage. But even then, they cannot prepare you for an unexpected accident, family crisis or national lockdown. However, plans can be changed and new pilgrimages will emerge. You can always still go somewhere, even in your imagination.

As far as walking the End to End was concerned, I started three years ahead of my 2019 pilgrimage by walking the Cleveland Way in North Yorkshire. At the time, I lived in West Yorkshire so it wasn't too far away. I could get to the start by public transport. It wouldn't take too long and I could carry a pack of things for about a week. In the end some adjustments were needed. I made use of a bag-carrying service for part of the route and eventually got a lighter rucksack. All these kinds of things are helpful to learn before doing the big one.

The year before the End to End I walked the Hadrian's Wall Path. This is a fantastic route and one I wholeheartedly recommend. There's even a bus to help you and the ends at Newcastle upon Tyne and Carlisle are readily accessible. It's easy to follow and includes some fascinating heritage and amazing views, but in the summer it was quite busy compared with some walks I've done.

It's likely that the Christian faith came to Britain with the Romans, although we don't know exactly how, and that it was spread by other missionaries after the Roman occupation ended. The Wall may not be the kind of monument we'd all want to celebrate, loudly declaiming empire and separation, but it does remind us of how the story of the crucified one first spread in this land.

Jesus said: 'Don't be fooled by stones, boys.' (RB)

I am not fooled by a line two thousand years old,
but I am a follower of the thread

that snakes the story across the land,
embedding it in communities,
changing lives
and I will celebrate that way.

2020 was a very different year. Travelling was restricted in Britain for much of the year and well into 2021. This meant repeated shorter routes and I was fortunate to have the Longdendale Valley on my doorstep. I'd repeat the same shorter routes almost daily and in the winter this was often only a mile at the most, but it was a comfort to see the water, the trees, the sky. I'd take photographs of the same spot, tree or rock and watch the scenery around change with the seasons. A daily pilgrimage on the same or similar routes is a good discipline. A small thing you notice one day may have been missed every day in the previous week. Equally, a slowly emerging plant or fungus can be admired each day as it changes over a period of time. Build those observations into your daily gratitude.

Most longer walks can be broken up into smaller sections. Often a guidebook or website will suggest these sections but you can readily make your own. On the West Highland Way my sections were about half or so of those recommended in the guides. I walked shorter days (around 8 to 10 miles), spent longer looking at things and sampling the local fare and thinking about what I was doing. I visited places of relevance to faith and life, from the Eden Project in the south-west to the Ruthwell Cross in the Borders to the RSPB centre at Forsinard Station in the Far North. That was all part of my pilgrimage. I go with the intention for holy encounter, with people, with the landscape, with creation and with the Travelling One.

May is National Walking Month but you can walk during most of the year in Britain, as long as you have a sense for your safety and that of others.

What to wear will depend on the length of the route and the level of challenge or difficulty. To a point, wear what you are comfortable with. I dislike gaiters and waterproof trousers, so I don't wear those. I have an old pair of trousers that dry out very quickly, and a blanket to wrap myself in at the end of the day if necessary. I have changed my wet trousers in odd places, including the layby north of the Kessock Bridge on the Black Isle after an absolute drenching while making the crossing. I still regard it as one of the wettest moments on my End to End.

You might want to take some sort of pilgrim sign with you. Some use the cockleshell of St James, which Sir Walter Raleigh mentions in his prayer 'Give me my cockle-shell of quiet'. Most of the long-distance walking routes in Britain have a badge or symbol to identify the route and you might like to use that as your sign. For example for the Pennine Way and some other long-distance routes it is the acorn; and each symbol you see can provide a thing to count as you progress.

22. Lost and found

Most of all to be avoided is getting lost. Some say getting lost is no bad thing, but that depends on the degree of lostness and the level of danger it involves. As I see it, there's a kind of Lostness Spectrum stretching from

no idea where I am or how to find out, in a dangerous situation …
to
the track is just over there, I have a compass and plenty of provisions.

It's important to be prepared for possible episodes of being lost, hence a map, compass and provisions. Depending on the length of the journey and the terrain, other resources may be needed: a jacket, an insulation blanket and so on. But I wouldn't take all that just to go up to the village shop.

Lost or not, I am still in your company.
Counting grains of sand or leaves on trees,
you outnumber me every time.
Awake or asleep you keep me close.
You find me and bring me home.

I did have a few 'lost' moments, once on a faint path through a heavy wood. But my biggest struggle was with the 'I can't do it' demon in my head. Most days I'd have a moment, at least, when I thought I'd not get to that day's end point. Indeed before I'd started I wasn't sure I'd get past the first week. The End to End is a huge undertaking, even in small sections, but then so is getting out of bed on some days.

Jesus said, 'Take your bed with you and go.' (RB)

Here in my bed,
here in the bed of a stream,
here in my head,
here at the head of a valley.
Here.
Here with you, Encourager.

Falling is another thing to avoid, unless you are very good at it. Falling off a wobbly stile in North Yorkshire resulted in a few stitches in my hand, and falling into a large number of nettles in East Yorkshire obviously left me well-stung. Test out stiles and admire nettles from a distance where possible. Have dock leaves to hand if stung (although some say this folk wisdom doesn't work).

Nettles are home to a host of species,
a welcome refuge for the smallest creature.
Don't disparage nettles: you can even eat them,
but a rash decision to take the nettle way
may result in a sting in more than your tail.

Feelings and emotions are an important part of pilgrimage. Take a measure of how you feel before you start. What emotions are you aware of? At Land's End I was aware of feeling empty, hollowed out. As I walked, feelings came back to me, sometimes in a rush, sometimes swirling through me, sometimes covering me in fog. I doubt two days of walking were the same as far as feelings and emotions were concerned. The business of remaking me was as long and hard as the walk itself, which had its own anxieties and doubts.

Tiredness also colours a walk. It could certainly ramp up my anxieties. Make sure you have enough with you to feed your hunger and pause when you need to rest. On a longer walk, like the End to End, be realistic about your pace and distance. Rest days or half days can be built in: a time to relax or explore in a different way.

Afterwards, it's important to tell it like it was. You may have a journal or blog to refer to or memories in other forms: a ferry ticket, a worn-through sole of a shoe … There will have been highs and lows, challenges and delights. Recall them as you can: such memories will also feed you.

In the Far North of Caithness in 2003, I saw the sunset behind a mountain and a herd of red deer crossed the road ahead of me. I stopped and drank it in, saying to myself, 'You'll need this when you get back.'

Praise God!
Give thanks: God is good and loves forever;
who can tell all the great things God has done?
Who can praise God enough? (RB)

I cannot praise you enough, God:
You have kept me safe and accompanied me.
Your love is communicated to me in so many ways:
I cannot give an adequate account of it.
I will continue to praise you;
I intend to travel your Way.

Part Two

Habits for habitats

The climate emergency did not emerge from nowhere but it has become more and more urgent. During 2019 while I was walking the End to End, Extinction Rebellion was taken up in the news, and schoolchildren around the world started to campaign for climate justice on Fridays. During the lockdowns in the UK in 2020 there was even more talk about the climate.

I know I was not the only person walking in the run-up to the global climate summit in Glasgow in November 2021. More and more organisations were trying to raise our awareness of the origins and effects of the climate crisis, particularly its effects on people of the Global South. The pandemic focused our attention on the fragile nature of the earth and all our connections. It was also interesting that a partial temporary global shutdown of polluting industries prodded us awake to how change could be possible. We began to talk about the 'new normal' and how 'green' that could be.

As I walked through Britain in 2019 I was hugely aware of green. Indeed I called the route my 'green ribbon' and reflected on how it unfurled as I went along. Travelling, listening, watching, I slowly made my way up the country, often recalling the names of the local species of plants and animals that I had learnt as a child. I walked through many different places and stopped and visited some that I'd wanted to see for a long time, like the Eden Project in Cornwall and the Slimbridge Wildfowl and Wetlands Trust Centre in Gloucestershire. I also passed places of high-density industrialisation, like Avonmouth, and some of the sites of our nuclear industry, like Reay on the Caithness coast. Occasionally I'd come across a local place of special scientific interest or a local Wildlife Trust site. It was these encounters that led me to organise this book around the habitats highlighted by the Wildlife Trust (www.wildlifetrusts.org/habitats): coastal, farmland, fresh water, grassland, heathland and moorland, marine, rocky habitat, towns and gardens, wetlands, woodland, some of which I've sub-divided or added to. Any of these habitats may be under threat for a range of reasons. Learning that the UK has only 53% of its biodiversity remaining (2021 figure) is shocking – it puts us in the bottom 10% of countries world-wide. Try to understand these things as part of your pilgrimage and con-sider what you can do to protect, respect and rewild.

I see myself as both activist and contemplative and recognise how important the balance is for my sustained engagement in climate issues. Activism is demanding and tiring: burnout is a real risk. And contempla-tion can become such a self-centred inward journey that we lose contact with the world: we cannot live on fish, chips and ice cream alone. Any journey through the landscape can bring us face to face with the demands of the climate change issues that confront us, as well as providing potential resources to rewild our onward journey. I hope you will annotate this col-lection with your own thoughts, experiences and prayers, both the things that challenge you and the things that encourage you.

How to use this book

You could use this book as part of your pilgrimage preparation.

You might want to take the prayers and meditations with you, and those offered here may inspire you to write your own.

When you return from your pilgrimage you'll want to think about it. Again, this guide can help. The stimulation of reading what someone else thought might help you to sift through your own thoughts, feelings and experiences.

If you are doing a virtual pilgrimage, then this book can be at your side.

If you are doing a day visit to one of these types of habitats, then this book might help open up new ideas about those places for you.

If you are engaged in an activity of protest, or are part of a group campaign, then some of the resources here may give you a breather, or help you to get ready for a next stage.

And if you are walking up the high street, this book may help you to experience it as a pilgrim way.

Wherever you journey, whatever you do, remember to 'Tread gently on the earth' (West African proverb).

1. Coast

I love the coast. Whichever way you do the End to End, whether you start at Land's End or John o'Groats, you are on the coast. In Britain, coast usually means wind – bracing weather which pushes you back or pulls you along. It can also mean cliffs, pebbles, islands, sand dunes, bays, harbours, rocks, lighthouses …

Wales has its own complete coast path and the England coast path is gradually joining up.

The coast can be a dangerous place. You may need knowledge of tides, for example, and cliffs and cliff-edges can crumble, so take care. Coastal erosion is very much a part of our landscape and makes our islands places of continual change.

Climate change has made coastlines more vulnerable, with higher tides and less predictable weather patterns. Lines of coastal defence are now more likely to be breached, putting roads and homes at risk in some places.

Coasts are places of great courage and bravery. The Penlee lifeboat *Solomon Browne* went down with all lives lost on the 19th December, 1981. A memorial on the South West Coast Path near Newlyn reminds the pilgrim of the crew's names and their dedication to 'Service Not Self'. As a pilgrim, I try to pause at memorials on the way when possible as a mark of respect.

A causeway is a safe place to cross,
but only for those who know the tides.

Only the Creator can tell how deep the water is;
as I look out, I cannot fathom it.

As waves mount up, so does my fear.
Christ can still the fiercest storm.

The Spirit calls us to acts of courage.
I stand by and remember.

Sand dunes

I've never seen a natterjack, though I did once see an adder, sliding through the sand.

I searched all over for a rare helleborine – and then found one on a local path.

As human activity encroaches on fragile habitats we displace the flora and fauna that flourish there. Stepping on sand dunes makes them slide.

May we be mindful of every step and tread gently on sand or earth.

Spurn Point

Spurn Point marks the end of Yorkshire in one way. At the end of the Holderness Coast, it's also a barometer for coastal erosion. In 2013 a storm washed over the causeway connecting the point to the mainland and the connection was severed, at least at the highest tides, making Spurn Point the newest tidal island in Britain. The point is a nature reserve and also contains the marks of various other coastal activities, particularly defence in the first half of the 20th century. You will also likely see a lot of ocean detritus on the shore, often lost pieces of fishing gear, nets and ropes and a great deal of plastic. A dead seal announced its presence via my nostrils, entangled as it was in ropes and nets.

Getting to the point
takes longer than you think.
How old will the young naturalists of today be
when we finally act for climate justice?
How long before we take the consequences of our acts seriously?
As the grains of sand are moved by the tides,
each one making a difference,
move us, Coast Creator,
to be people of action rather than drift.

Loch Fleet

Loch Fleet, a tidal sea-water loch on the north-east coast of Scotland, is an RSPB nature reserve. In the 19th century, Christian missionaries to Greenland, translating the Lord's Prayer into an Inuit language, used the phrase 'Give us our daily seal', as bread was unknown in the Inuit culture. I often pray to see a daily seal, balancing banana-like on the rocks, when I am on the coast.

Silence may be fleeting,
or it may last and last and last.
As the tide ebbs and flows
I let the silence flow around me,
lap at my bootlaces,
seep through my cagoule.
If only I could spend all day
balancing like a seal,
content in my skin.

Salt marsh

On the edge of the land and sea you may find salt marsh, a flat landscape that invites and repels the tides. Infiltrated by inlets, this fragile land is sometimes grazed (lamb raised on salt marsh is said to develop a particular flavour) but mostly it is left to wildlife: waders, floaters and flyers, both native and visiting species, and specialist plants that can withstand the saltiness.

Without salt, this marshland would not be so distinctive.
Without salt, our pilgrim lives would be bland.

We need salt in our marsh and salt in our lives
if we are to make the world salty enough.

Coastal mist

Watch out for changes in the weather. On the coast, sea mist is a potential
hazard, as it was on the north coast of Caithness when I walked it in 2019.

The sea may be blue at times,
but when the mist rolls in,
even though it's still there,
it's hard to see the sea.
Sound and smell take over
as the fog creates a different world.
May we, with our heads in the clouds,
tread surely, gently and firmly,
rooted to the earth
for which you made us.

Welcome

Sometimes a welcome is unexpected. I'm not a golf person. I often pass
golf courses, especially on the coast, where the land naturally gives itself
to greens and bunkers and I believe the game originated. Most are for
members only, which rather cuts them off from the passing pilgrim. Reay
Golf Club on the north coast of Caithness was not like that, and on a wet
and windy day its hospitality was very welcome.

Not golf-related

I'm not a golf-related traveller,
although I know the green.
I'm not a golf-related traveller,
although I stop for tea.
I can swing and drive,
and always have plenty of irons in the fire,
but the clubhouse on a misty day
was my most welcome spot
in a golf-related way.

Of course the largest 'golf ball' at Reay is at Dounreay, the nuclear power station that is undergoing a decommissioning process. You may walk past other nuclear power stations, both active and being decommissioned, depending on the route you take.

This power, product of the interaction of the tiniest particles,
may seem seductively simple;
but cleaning up is hugely complicated.
Can any generation really count the cost?
May we not be fooled by the isolated location
into thinking this won't cost the earth,
but value it all, remembering the tiniest coastland species,
and not just the bits we think we can exploit.

Activities for pilgrims on the coast

Coasts are especially vulnerable to climate change. What signs of threat from climate change do you see around you? Look for the high tideline. Where does it reach up to? Do you see signs that the coastline is changing due to higher tides, for example cliff falls or erosion of sand dunes. Are there notices warning people of these possible events?

What kinds of things are being thrown up by the tide?

Write or draw in the damp sand or make a sand castle or sculpture or map.

Make a pattern or message with pebbles or shells.

Feel the sand between your toes or fingers or the water lapping your feet or hands.

Look into a rock pool at the tiny world there.

Join a beach clean-up or litter-pick (you may need particular equipment for this).

Leave only footprints.

2. Mountains and moorland

Psalm 121 is an ideal psalm in uplands or lowlands, and is also known as the Traveller's Psalm.

Here's a remembered version:

Look up at the hills:
the restless Creator
keeps watch from there,
and never dozes off. (RB)

I'm restless too, as I march on.
The hills beckon and entice me.
May I be prepared,
have enough breath to catch
and muscles to leg it.

There are many accessible upland places in Britain, and some much less accessible ones. Such places can be bleak and travellers may become vulnerable in changeable weather. Ben Nevis is the highest mountain in Britain. I've not climbed it but I've been near enough to see others making the attempt, moving ant-like up the steep sides. Mostly I admire mountains from the bottom.

Crack of light

A silver nick,
a lightening tick,
cracks through the cloud
all thundering down
the distant hills.
The ragged edge,
like a whiskered hedge,
parts silently
enough to see
the promised good.

Passes

I call out to God, who answers me from the holy mountain.
I lie down and sleep and I wake up again, because God keeps me going.
(RB)

When walking in the mountains I often yearn to come upon a pass. A passage through to the next valley is a welcome sight, providing a moment of respite after the toil of trudging and climbing up, a moment to rest, to appreciate the view (if you can see it) and anticipate the descent.

Just passing,
I whisper
to the God of justice,
peace and hope.

The Lairig Mor

The Lairig Mor, on the West Highland Way, means 'Large Pass', and is reputed to be the escape route used by the MacGregors in 1645 when they were trying to outrun the Campbells. There are steep rocky slopes on each side and quite a few streams to ford.

Even though I walk through Death's valley, I am not afraid, for you are there for me. (RB)

When I walk, waves of anxiety may come and go with me, mostly due to over-thinking. There is so much in life that we cannot control. Jesus doesn't avoid Death's valley; and being familiar with the landscape is ready to walk through it again with us.

The Devil's Staircase

Folk do wonder about this section of the West Highland Way and I've been asked about it by other walkers. I wonder why there are so many 'satanic' landmarks in Britain: the Devil's Beeftub in the Southern Uplands, the Devil's Elbow in Derbyshire, and on the West Highland Way, the Devil's Staircase.

The path from the valley near Altnafeadh on the Glencoe side curves steeply upwards, and as I was walking I could see my ant-like companions zigzagging backwards and forwards higher up the climb. It's the sort of walk where you get to recognise each other, passing individuals and groups on the ascent as you rest and walk, walk and rest, all the way up. But, as far as I know, I didn't meet the Devil. I can imagine that travellers from earlier times may have been very wary of climbs like this, particularly in bad weather, hence the name. Rather than a Devil's Staircase, it had me in mind of Jacob's dream of a ladder stretching between earth and heaven, with angels going up and down.

As ants collaborate to make life easier,
so walkers need to work in harmony
to ascend the heights or travel over rough ground.

From the top of a mountain, you were shown the world.
As we admire the view, may we be as sure-footed
in our pursuit of the route to your kindom, Mountain Walker.

There's a route on the Pennine Way in Derbyshire that actually includes a feature called Jacob's Ladder, which is a set of stone steps cut into a hillside leading up onto the Kinder Plateau. This area is especially rich in archaeological features, with tumuli of different sizes scattered across the hills, indicating just how sacred this upland landscape was to our Neolithic and Bronze Age ancestors. Salisbury Plain is another area rich in such signs, as are the Orkney Islands. Before setting out as a pilgrim, study maps to understand the ways, routes and landmarks of our forebears, so you can spot them when you are on the ground.

The line, this mound, these stones:
other pilgrims came this way in the past,
and considered it holy.
May I show the same respect today.

The Flow Country

On day 111 of the End to End I took the route across the Flow Country. One of my main reasons for walking this way, apart from avoiding the A9, was to cross this largest area of blanket bog in the world and UNESCO World Heritage Site. Covering some 4000 square kilometres of Caithness and Sutherland in northern Scotland, it supports an important diversity of species. It is one of the places where the blanket bog moss sphagnum actively works to ensure peat accumulation, making it an important resource in terms of climate change, locking in carbon. Other wetland plants, like sundew and butterwort, also thrive here.

My walk started at the junction near Kinbrace Station on a bright morning. I was walking along the same road as the previous day, but along this stretch there were fewer signs of human habitation, both ancient and recent. A train went past on the Far North Line and the views of Loch an Ruathair were lovely. Bob met me before the summit of the pass to Forsinard. Not long after that it started raining.

We saw the rain clouds sweeping across the Flow and as a result of the wind direction my right leg was getting wetter than my left. Bob had mentioned the Forsinard station café and as we were already quite wet it seemed a good place to dry off. There was a sheep guarding the door but we managed to get inside. Its simple menu required extensive sampling and I'm glad to report that the soup, scones and chocolate cake were all excellent. The sheep kept guard while we ate, even dozing off on the porch. We dried out as thunder rumbled on around us.

During a brief break in the weather we walked down to the station where the RSPB have an exhibition about the Flow Country and its importance as a bird reserve. Various migrant birds and important resident species can be seen in this wild open country and viewed from a nearby lookout tower.

The rain and thunder began again. We sat inside until it cleared up and then I legged it down the road for a further mile, until the rain began again, blowing in waves across the Flow Country, keeping it wet and wild for now.

Thunder is glorious: it is God rumbling over the ocean. (RB)

Cosmic Creator, the laws of physics make for an amazing universe:
We are in awe of phenomena like thunder.
We acknowledge that rain makes the Flow Country what it is
and we know blanket bog is an important habitat.
Surely, the connections between all of these physical aspects of the world
echo the complexity of the Holy Three: Creator, Son and Spirit.

Moorland

There are other upland areas to explore on the End to End, particularly Bodmin Moor, Dartmoor and Exmoor in the southwest, and the Pennines in the North of England. Because of their less accessible nature they often retain many ancient features: barrows, ancient tracks or paths and stone crosses for example. However, they are also susceptible to damage, particularly from wildfires. Do not light fires on moorland – leave your barbecue at home.

As the road rises and falls,
as the hills mount in waves to the horizon,

as the track winds downhill
or climbs steeply to the summit,
so I am amazed to be walking this way.
The cross marks the way;
both guide and meeting point,
telling part of the human story in this landscape.
With a buzzard's-eye view of the earth,
or a primrose-eye view from the hedge,
keep us in your care, Creator.
May the road rise to meet us.

Activities for pilgrims on mountains and moorland

For all their looming size and extent, moorlands and mountains can be vulnerable to climate change. Here are some signs of the effects of climate change to look out for: moorland areas drying and shrinking; more erosion on upland paths as they dry out or are washed out by repeated fiercer cycles of extreme weather; less evidence of specialist moorland species of plants, mosses and lichens; upland animal species that change the colour of their coats or plumage for winter (mountain hares, stoats and ptarmigan) visible on the hills where snow no longer lies in winter.

Add a stone to any cairn you may pass en route.

Look out for the creatures and plants of the moors and mountains: white hares in winter, curlews and other ground-nesting birds in summer …

Admire the view from a trig point, a white triangular post used for mapping purposes.

At night a moorland may offer wide views of the night sky.

Breathe as deeply and slowly as you can.

Do no damage.

3. Routes

I prefer to walk on traffic-free routes, but that is not always possible. Sometimes it's necessary to cross from one trail or path to another using a section of roadway, or a path may be closed for maintenance, resulting in a rerouting. A very wet day on the Severn Way meant that the next day I opted for the footway along the A38, which was drier. Even there the verges had their orchids and other flowering plants. Verges, service stations, canal towpaths and tunnels can all be part of a pilgrim route, although some might be noisier than the peaceful pilgrim would prefer. It's important to encounter the world as it is on such a journey, to remind us of what needs to be challenged or changed. Wear a high-visibility vest or jacket when on roadways.

The traffic snarls, surrounding me like the Bulls of Bashan.
Sharp bends and the cresting hills obscure my view.
When there is no footway I rely on drains and ditches as places of refuge.
Even though this is a challenging way, I reach the end.
Wisdom ushers me along,
making sure I seek clear sight-lines and sensible places to cross.
I am delivered from traffic, noise and stress
and the flower-lined green lanes return to guide me home.

I love the reference to the Bulls of Bashan in Psalm 22.

If you are concerned about walking through cattle, as some are, then think ahead. A friend planning to do a long-distance walk did a 'cattle awareness walk' with a local farmer that helped her to feel more confident before she started.

I emerged from a path into a farmyard in Cornwall – with plenty of mud and young cattle. I stuck to the far edge of the yard and they watched me pass by. The farmer also saw me and came out to greet me, escorting me to the gate and the next section of path. As we entered the last section of the yard he patted a larger bull on the rump and encouraged him to move out of our way: so much for the Bulls of Bashan, I thought.

Canals

Canals were once the arteries of industrial Britain. They are now mostly quieter leisure routes. I enjoy walking the towpaths, even if they are often a rather roundabout way of getting somewhere. The Leeds and Liverpool Canal, for example, is not at all direct as the crow would fly. Nor are canals always flat. In some places staircases of locks, like at Neptune's Staircase on the Caledonian Canal at Banavie, are required to gain the necessary height. Remember that if you are travelling by kayak or canoe you must remove your craft from the water at a lock flight. A portage sign, two figures with a canoe on their head, will usually indicate this.

On the waterways, as the scenery slips by,
where the waterfowl nurture their young,
so you restore me.
I am made new by each step;
each sight refreshes me;
I am remade by the Maker through the beauty of creation.

The speed of travelling concerns some, but I try not to give it much thought. (However, it can be important to have an idea of your capacity to complete a route and have options available for ending it sooner if circumstances change.)

I was walking alongside the Shropshire Union Canal, slow-going canal boats passing me, when I wrote this next piece. Travelling by canal was considered fast at the beginning of the Industrial Revolution. I take between twenty and forty minutes for a mile, depending on how distracted I happen to be or how steep the route.

I wonder how slow is slow?
As I speed along
can I even wait for ice cream to melt,
or see the grass growing?
I yearn for the slow lane,
as long as it's not that slow:
Wondering at you, God,
your slow emotions, your limitless love.

As one step gives way to the next,
keep me alongside you,
Generous Companion.

The Anderton Boat Lift is just one amazing water-powered piece of engineering on our canal network. Linking the River Weaver Navigation to the Trent and Mersey Canal, it has been restored and operates for vertical pilgrimages.

Lifted up,
cradled in a watery embrace,
this feat of engineering,
the work of human beings
by hand and brain,
gives a whole new perspective on the world.
May our pilgrimage today,
in the company of the Cosmic Engineer,
be uplifting and awesome.

Canal tunnels or tunnels on disused railway lines may be subject to specific rules too. You can walk through some. Others you have to walk over. Long or short, they are a good reason to have a head-torch with you if you intend to walk through, as the walking surface may be damp or uneven or both. It's always good to see the light at the end of any tunnel.

From the dark of the tunnel
the boat emerges into the light of day;
every day has its contrasts:
the warmth of the sun and the cold wind;
the quiet canal and the noisy motorway;
walking by myself or together;
eating alone or with others.

May we embrace the possibilities that you offer us,
the new life you hold out to us
each day.

Fly-tipping

Sadly too many of the routes I've taken through Britain are subjected to increased fly-tipping. The local council will usually have a helpline or website where you can report fly-tipping finds.

Wind down that window, chuck this out;
open the boot, dump this here;
draw up your truck, heave these over the edge:
Fly-tipping is the sort of day-tripping we can all do without.

All-knowing God, who sees what we do in public and in secret,
help us to face up to our responsibilities as residents of this planet.
It matters what we do with its resources and the rubbish we generate.
Hold us to account.

Service stations

Strangely enough, a pilgrim can usually walk into a motorway service station, by the back door so to speak. I visited several such service stations on the End to End. I walked into both Tebay and Southwaite services on the M6, another by the Severn Bridge, stayed at the A76 services at Kilmarnock and more recently walked into Tibshelf services on the M1 after a visit to the village chippy. Each one had its treasures and toilets. At Kilmarnock services there were a lot of common spotted-orchids.

Between the busy roads and junctions,
where heavy traffic passes,
these small oases have many functions,
feeding people and wildlife.
I count the orchids in one, the butterflies in another;
ducks make their presence felt
as motorists watch their sandwiches.
Let's face it, we all need a break.

Verge prayer

'Please do not cut the verge: wild flowers' (Notice on a verge in Cumbria)

On the edge of the road, on the edge of extinction:
take care of the edge and those that live there,
green things and other creatures:
take care of the edges and we will all thrive.
May those on the verge of change be converted to edge-lovers.

'No Mow May' has become a movement to let verges, meadows and gardens grow during the spring flowering season. It urges mowers not to cut until after such plants have set their seed, in an attempt to rewild and diversify our countryside.

No one went to mow,
went to mow in May,
no one mowed and so
there's more plants next May.
(*Sung to the tune of 'One man went to mow'*)

Plague stones

Past plagues have also left their mark on our routes. During earlier centuries, versions of social distancing rules required plague stones to be put up in places to enable people to exchange goods more safely. The idea was that you left your money or goods at the plague stone. The stone had a shallow depression in the top surface which was filled with vinegar to allow for the safe exchange of currency. There's one by the A6 on the way into Penrith.

When a rampant disease threatens lives
a community needs to pull together.
This stone is witness to decisions made in earlier times.
Today we still need to protect each other and live safely,
even if 'click and collect' has replaced the vinegar.
May visitors breathe easy in this space.

Road maintenance

There's a whole lot to do …
Routes ages-old
linking community to community,
making a network for work and leisure, life and death:

Travelling One, we remember the roads we've travelled,
those who travel with us, before us and behind.
May we develop routes safely:
not disturbing ancient aquifers
or cropping the highways of smaller species.
May we do so mindful of those who maintain these highways
so helping to keep us connected.

Activities for pilgrims on different routes

Routes can have both positive and negative consequences, for communities, for species and for the climate. As you travel, think about this.

Count bridges or locks on canals, as they are often numbered.

Watch people working the locks or at the roadworks.

Look out for what does survive along roadways and verges.
Use honesty boxes honestly.
Share the limited space on towpaths with care and respect.
Leave no litter.

4. Woodland

When the going was hard, I cried out to God, who brought me into a spacious place. (RB)

Woodland is one of my favourite habitats – any time of the year. Britain was once mostly covered with woodland. Now only a small portion of that ancient woodland remains. Some will argue that new woodlands have been planted; but these cannot immediately replace ancient woodland – the clue is in the name.

Some of our woodland planting has been controversial, for example extensive conifer cultivation with non-native species, and is now being reversed. Woodland has also become a political football, with what is said about respecting woodland and what is done often being far apart in the public arena. Ancient woodland is said to be important, whilst at the same time it is carved up for dubious infrastructure projects.

Whichever kind of woodland you visit, try to use your senses to explore what you find. Woodland is a great place for scent and texture, so employ what senses you can on your travels, or ask a companion to do this for you and to report their findings. Woodland is rarely a silent place and each will have its own soundscape. There's nothing quite like standing under the green cathedral of a canopy of leaves knowing that the trees are doing something you can't do, for free, that is essential to life on earth.

Woodland can reward repeated pilgrimages to the same place as the seasons change. It can also provide a spot for meditation, forest-bathing (a way of just being in the forest) or tree-hugging: all ways of getting in touch with the full atmosphere of the forest.

Woodland is the place where I get nearest to the Native American understanding: 'When I walk, I walk in beauty.'

Temperate rainforest

You may still find small fragments of this in fringe places: the Ardnamurchan Peninsula in western Scotland, the forests of the Eryri/Snowdonia National Park in North Wales, and in some of the deeper, smaller Derbyshire Dales, like Monk's Dale, for example. Temperate rainforest is characterised by dampness and epiphytes, which are plants that grow on other plants but are not parasitic (e.g. ferns).

Should I take this woodland track,
worn by footsteps, ages old?
Should I enjoy the shelter of this canopy:
the millions of cells working to harness sunlight,
the birds calling and creatures crawling?
How well I know that you speak to us through the wood,
each annual ring an endorsement of constancy.
The fallen leaves of many years make this path
as I add my footsteps to those already here.

Young woodland

There's currently a great drive to plant new trees and nurture young woodlands across Britain. It's timely, and also takes time. Young woodland does
not mature overnight; it takes centuries to become ancient woodland.
Young woodland is hope for the future.

Little shoot, little leaf,
growing, growing, growing.

Find something small to admire:
a nut or fruit,
a leaf or twig.
Touch it gently.
Hold it on your open palm.
Consider its story,
what it is to grow and mature,
the time it takes and
the route ahead.

View from the Great Glen Way

The landscape keeps on changing. The sheltering trees give way to heather moorland. Loch Ness glitters in the sunlight. Small streams jump down the rocks. The trees come back: this is young, recently planted woodland. It is wonderful to see. And in the midst of it is a small eco-café with a tasty menu!

For what we are about to enjoy
may we be truly thankful,
mindful of the place and the taste,
the work and the hospitality.

Ancient Caledonian pine forest

This still exists in some remote parts of Scotland. One such place is the Balblair Woods on the north shore of Loch Fleet. At different times of the year you may find rare plants here: in spring, the one-flowered wintergreen, and in autumn, lady's tresses, a species of British orchid.

I kneel reverently, breathing softly,
joining the invertebrates in homage
to the dainty woodland dwellers.

Special trees

Any tree is a special tree. Choose one and get to know it well. It will quite possibly be home for thousands of other species. There are named trees in various parts of Britain: the Chained Oak near Alton in Staffordshire, the Major Oak in Sherwood Forest, the Bethnal Green Mulberry are just a few.

The Chained Oak in Staffordshire is the subject of several old myths. You can visit the tree readily. It's on a path near Alton Towers theme park and it really does have chains holding it together, although some branches of the tree have now fallen away. It's an amazing tree, standing sentinel in its chains.

Chained to stop it falling,
chained to limit its life;
the chained oak represents
the way we chain up the world,
limiting its capacity to regenerate
and nurture other species.
May we loosen the chains we impose
and seek a way of thriving together.

Activities for pilgrims in woodlands

Trees and woodlands absorb carbon dioxide, a major greenhouse gas, and also provide shelter and homes for many species: look for nests and holes. A nurse log is an old dead piece of tree that is decaying and providing nutrients to fungi and the soil.

There are many woodland specialists: fungi of different sizes, woodland birds like woodpeckers and treecreepers. Which do you notice?

Look for epiphytes, plants that grow on other plants but are not parasitic.

How many colours of green can you see? Can you think of names for all the different shades?

Foraging has become popular, but try to forage with your eye or your camera rather than pick stuff, even if it looks abundant. If you do pick something, make sure it's only sufficient for your own needs, and isn't poi-sonous. Treat any foraged items like manna in the wilderness: don't be greedy.

Try not to remove anything from the woodland, as any organic matter may make an important contribution to the habitat.

Look out for items nibbled by other creatures and try to work out who they might be.

Celebrate the lives of any trees, standing or felled: their rings may be counted or you can put your arms around the trunk to estimate their age.

Use as many senses as you can to take in the woodland atmosphere. Ask a companion to share their sensory feedback with you if you have sensory limitations.

At the end of any walk in woodland, please adhere to local guidelines concerning plant health. In some areas plant diseases are a serious threat and pilgrims need to ensure they are not unwittingly transmitting these to other places. If local advice includes cleaning your boots on leaving a site, please ensure you do.

5. Wetlands and marshes

Some parts of Britain have always been wetter than others. Standing at Gold Corner on the Somerset Levels where there is a pumping station, you can see, above its doorway, a mark for the extent of flooding in the past. Its height suggests that it was indeed entirely surrounded by water. By the time I got to Gold Corner myself, I was entirely saturated by the rain.

In the silver-grey light of a dense mist,
it's hard to see Gold Corner,

where the water has sometimes been higher than my head.
In the knee-high grass and flowers, as the rain seeps in,
it's hard to be grateful for a walk in the wet land.
As the frog croaks, so I croak out my gratitude,
for the wet land and the way ahead.

Slimbridge

There are a number of Wildfowl and Wetland Trust reserves across Britain, of which Slimbridge in Gloucestershire, founded by Sir Peter Scott, is probably the best known. Caring for vulnerable places like wetlands is important in supporting species and vulnerable people and communities worldwide, as we struggle to meet the challenge of keeping the world in balance. Many migratory wetland species rely on our end of the wetland habitat chain for their survival. They may come from the Arctic tundra, which is warming, and need the security of a nesting area to raise the next generation. Indigenous people in these areas rely on the migratory geese for down, amongst other things. Our wetlands are part of a global chain. The Wildfowl and Wetlands Trust is involved in research studies to promote understanding of the complexities of bird migration.

Jesus said: 'Oh, Jerusalem, how I wish I could gather you up like a hen gathers her chicks.' (RB)

As the birds call to each other at the end of the day,
flocking to a safe roost,
so we gather close to you, our God.
Like a mother bird you shelter us.
May we mirror your care in the way we relate to others,
particularly vulnerable people.

Bird sanctuary

On the John o'Groats Trail, on the dunes past Brora alongside the golf course, there's a sign to remind the walker of the nesting Arctic terns. Not that they let you forget their presence – even when you keep your distance. But who can blame them? They have a long journey too, much longer than mine, and only have a short season to nest and raise their young before heading back again.

The coast of Britain is an important place for many breeding seabirds. The human coronavirus pandemic has been followed by an avian flu pandemic that has decimated many seabird colonies. If you come across dead birds, do not touch the carcasses.

Support the work of bird protection organisations in any way you can: a regular subscription or a slice of cake at the nature reserve café all play their part.

God will cover you with his feathers, and under his wings you will find refuge. (RB)

The cormorants hang their wings out to dry.
A feather or two blows across the sand.
The Arctic terns spin in the air, clattering a noisy warning.
These are the birds that God has counted,
whose feathered wings provide a refuge.

God bless us in the air:
the air we breathe,
the air we share.

Rewilding prayer

There's a lay-by on the A9 near Lothbeg where we have stood as a family many times. A memorial stone there recalls the death of the last she-wolf in Sutherland, which was killed near there over three hundred years ago. Since then there have been no wild wolves in Sutherland, but there are plans for rewilding, and not only with wolves. Beavers, wildcats, sea eagles and others are also talked of.

How it must irk you, Creator,
when we limit the habitats of your precious ones.
How it must sorrow you, Son,
when there is no wilderness, no place to escape to.
How it must grieve you, Spirit,
when our human spirits are so far removed from the care of our kin.
Remembering the roamers, the endangered ones and the dreamers:
may we be changed, one cell at a time,
to rewilders, makers of place and space,
sharers of the interwoven global kindom,
in the name and power of the Holy and all-abiding Three.

Reservoirs

We live in the Longdendale Valley in north Derbyshire. In the 19th century the valley was changed by the construction of a chain of reservoirs to provide water to the growing city of Manchester. Those changes have now become part of the landscape and are welcome refuges for wildlife. You may share the path with a deer at dawn or twilight, see bats dance in the air as darkness falls, hear an owl or a cuckoo or curlew. At certain times of the year the valley provides a migrating route for pink-footed geese, who honk their way across the sky in long skeins, calling out encouragement to each other. In 2020, at the height of the pandemic, the valley was home to a bearded vulture, a lammergeier. Probably from the Alps, it spent several weeks in the valley as a tourist and raised our spirits considerably.

Soar on, high-flying one.
Uplifted by air currents,
carried by weather patterns,
homed on high crags,
we welcome you.
May we welcome human beings as enthusiastically.

Activities for pilgrims visiting wetlands and marshes

How wet are the wetlands? In periods of prolonged drought wetlands are likely to dry out, whilst in wetter periods they may flood.

If possible, spend some time in a wildlife hide and see what you notice. It may be quite a common species, but quiet observation can help us to notice something previously missed, perhaps its particular colours, or the way it moves.

Depending on the weather, watery places can provide a mirror that reflects the earth and sky. You can see the world inverted even in a puddle in the right circumstances. Look out for a wet place in which to reflect and see the world differently.

Touch water gently – or wear boots for a bigger splash. Float a twig or leaf in a puddle.

Take part in some counting activity. Even quite common species need our care.

Remember not to leave bird feeders out for too long without a thorough clean-out as they can harbour viruses that are dangerous to avian visitors.

Take care when searching for vulnerable species.

6. Rivers and estuaries

The River Severn is 220 miles long and is the longest river in Britain. The Severn Way follows the river and the route's waymark is a sailing boat in a white circle. In 2019, I began it at Avonmouth and continued to Ironbridge in Shropshire, although the Severn Way does continue to the source of the Severn in Wales. The way is not always a useable route as the Severn is increasingly prone to flooding in some sections, so check this out before you start.

The path moves from one bank to the next, depending on crossing places. At the estuary end it is very wide and tidal. As I worked my way upriver, it gradually narrowed, but even by Ironbridge was still wide and a mighty force, especially in flood conditions.

There are many places on the Severn Way to pray and reflect. The poet and composer of songs Ivor Gurney (1890–1937), remembered in Gloucester Cathedral, wrote about the meadows of the River Severn: 'Do not forget me quite, O Severn meadows …'

Gurney served in the trenches of the First World War, and suffered from bipolar disorder throughout his life; his last fifteen years were spent in a psychiatric hospital. His gravestone is in the churchyard of Twigworth Parish Church in Gloucestershire.

The meadows of the River Severn, as it winds through Gloucestershire, are indeed lovely. Watch the light change and the wind ripple through the trees and long grass. Listen to the sounds around you, or ask someone to describe them to you. These things are beautifully portrayed in the windows of Gloucester Cathedral.

For those who prefer a smaller sanctuary, Odda's Chapel on the banks near Deerhurst is one of the oldest complete chapels in Britain, having been built in 1056 before the Norman Conquest, possibly by a relative of Edward the Confessor. It is only a few steps from the path, and its bare simplicity is well worth a prayerful pause.

The meadows around the chapel were quite wet, the long grass soaking my trousers, the plants heavily nodding to me as I passed. Once I'd left the shelter of the chapel, the only dry place to pause and ponder in the extensive meadows was under the motorway bridge.

The dry grass, the brown earth:
signs of the rain we need.
The floodgates and water-height indicators:
signs of the conflict between humanity and environment.
For centuries human industry and the flow of the river
have striven to keep pace here.

In our generation we need the wisdom
to maintain a healthy balance for all creation.
In your mercy, empower us to make mindful decisions
for a sustainable world.

Since 2012, the Canal and River Trust has been responsible for over two thousand miles of waterways in England and Wales. It has a band of volunteers who help to keep things flowing. Where a river has previously been in spate you may see a line of materials, often including plastic, hung up on the branches of trees along the banks. Rubbish like this and other litter can clog up a river or canal.

As the water glides by there are many signs of its earlier activity:
the debris caught in roots and branches,
the rock cliffs and muddy paths,
the weirs, locks and bridges still working today.
Walking through the green,
I pray for the people who draw life from the waterway
for both work and leisure.

Floods

Your path led through the sea, your way through huge floods, though your footprints were invisible. (RB)

There has been a lot of work on flood defences, not just along the Severn Way but in other parts of the End to End, and still some places, like Northwich town centre in January 2021, have flooded. This has become a more regular and alarming occurrence and has led climate scientists to state that climate change is not something that will occur in the future, but is already here.

Where places flood, folk may be cut off,
waiting for waters to subside or for routes to be restored.
Animals may be marooned, fields inundated
and livelihoods put at risk.
People may find themselves taking great risks.
Christ, have mercy.

Where people live on floodplains:
an isolated farm, a new development, a traveller site,
may we be mindful of the gamble we take
with their lives and livelihoods.
Christ, have mercy.

Bridges

Bridges are important places of reflection for pilgrims. Crossing over from one place to another, they often mark progress on a route or a transition from one landscape to another, and may also help a walker to avoid a much longer route. Each bridge is an amazing feat of engineering in its own unique way.

The Three Lochs Way in Argyll was part of my End to End in 2019. Not a route we had used before, it was quite strenuous in places. The Dave Markland Bridge there is named in memory of a Warrant officer who managed the development of the Gurkha Bato in Argyll, which was built by Gurkha engineers, and which was opened as part of a route for long-distance walkers in 2010. Dave Markland was sadly killed in action in Afghanistan in 2010. We ate our lunch by this bridge.

Crossing over a few planks,
walking on an even path,

sharing sandwiches in the wild.
For what we are about to receive,
may we be truly thankful
and mindful of those who made it possible.

At the Bridge of Oich on the Great Glen Way there's a warning notice that states that only a maximum of fifty people are allowed on the historic bridge at any one time. Warning: do not overload the bridge.

It may swing and sway or even give way.
Warning: do not overload the planet.
It will overheat, sea levels rise, species go extinct.
Can't you see the signs?

Other ways of crossing a river

There may be other safe ways of crossing a stream or river. Some places have stepping stones or clapper bridges that are centuries old, like at Tarr Steps on the River Barle, or at Bolton Abbey. In other places they may have been placed recently to cope with changes in the course of the river or water levels. A ford will sometimes be accompanied by a depth guide, as at Kempsey Church on the River Severn, but not always.

Stepping stones in Chee Dale

I may be out of my depth
as I size up these stones
and consider my options,
but a safe crossing
gives me such a positive feeling:
I made it, I got across.

Activities for pilgrims visiting rivers and estuaries

When visiting rivers, what do you notice? Debris, often plastic, on the bank or in trees indicates how high a river rises. An empty riverbed may indicate that the river has gone underground, as can happen in Limestone Country.

Are there nests for birds and animals in sheltered places?

What is the water like: clear or murky? What can you see in the water? Is the cleanliness of the water commented on? Blue-green algae blooms are increasingly common in some rivers and are a danger to people and wildlife.

Look for interesting reflections or patterns.

Play Pooh sticks from a bridge.

If there are some safe stepping stones or an old clapper bridge, cross over (carefully). Watch the way the water flows around the stones. This activity is not advisable for unaccompanied children, those with mobility limitations or when a river is in spate.

Look for flood marks on bridges or riverside buildings. Respect flood defences.

Look out for river specialists like the dipper or the kingfisher.

7. Agricultural land

From the very first steps of my End to End in 2019 to the last, I was walking alongside or across agricultural land. Hedgerows, meadows, orchards, farmyards, crop fields, grazing land – there are so many different ways in which the land is marked by agriculture.

Let all creatures praise God –
even the young inquisitive cattle!
Let all wild flowers praise God –
like jewels in every hedge!
Let all birds praise God –
wading egrets and soaring buzzards!
Let everything created praise God.

Through rutted field and along muddy track,
let all living things praise God.

Gates

Jesus said, 'I am the gate for the sheep.' (RB)

Any Way will have plenty of gates, some open, some closed, some easier
to open or close than others. What is the purpose of a gate, other than to
go through it?

Pause at each gate.
Weigh the gate as it opens and closes.
See how it fits into the space or not.
Give the gate time to swing.
Observe any notices on the gate.

If Jesus is the gate, then it's not for us to take up gatekeeping.

Lambing shed prayer

Lambing season is a very busy time as each new life is midwifed into the world. Be aware of lambs in the fields and any other livestock.

May you have bright crisp nights
and see the stars above you.
May the wind be gentle
and the owls good company.
May the barn stand firm
and all your hands be welcoming
as new life slips into the world.

Honey

Your words taste so sweet – sweeter than honey in my mouth! (RB)

The bees are very busy and the meadows and verges are alive with their buzzing. Each flower makes an inviting place for a bee: foxglove and dog rose, each one a cup for a bee to drink from. The golden nectar that the bees collect is a special bounty, replaying the taste of summer on our lips. It's no wonder that ancient people likened this liquor to God's words. Honey will taste of the nectar of the flowers from which it is collected, and so vary in flavour at different times of the year. It's well worth comparing some different ones to enjoy this seasonal delight.

Rain

Like rain falling on a mown field, like showers watering the earth, that is
how God is. (RB)

We see the rain as it approaches from the coast:
Grey clouds bubble up, streaks fall like curtains;
the grass bends and a hard shower peppers the road.
Afterwards, when the sun comes out,
steam rises like a hot spring, or the surface of a bath.
So we are changed when God touches us,
our communities transformed by the movement of the Holy Spirit.

Green

Green marks Ordinary Time,
but green is not at all ordinary.
In any landscape there is so much that's green:
between the cracks, alongside the tracks,
covering the hills, beside the rills.
Gladness and joy overflow in me
as I walk through the green.

Green is not the only colour in an agricultural landscape of course. Look
out for all the other colours too: the yellow of rapeseed plants, the blue of
flax ... Orchards blossoming with different-coloured flowers in spring ...

Thank you for the trees in blossom.
Thank you for the pink and white.
Thank you that they bloom in springtime
making quite a sight.

Community orchards

A community orchard is a wonderful way to create a space and share resources. I've visited them in towns and in the countryside. A well-placed seat in one can make for a restful oasis. Growing items locally helps to cut down on food miles.

From blossom to fruit,
may we share the labour,
savouring the sweetness
after the work of the harvest.

Wild flowers

The grass dries up and the flowers fade, but what God says lasts forever (RB)

There's a movement to increase wild flower meadows – and it's gaining ground.

You dare to cut us down, but we spring back up again.
You uproot us, drench us in pesticides – but still we rise!
We are the wild ones peppering the landscape:
Join us!

How many wild flowers do you know the names of? Many have particular local names as well as their more common names. Monk's hood is a striking dark-blue plant from a family of plants called aconites, which are poisonous (particularly their roots). It has many other names, including wolf's bane, and is thought to have been used in ancient times to kill wolves. I saw this rather sinister plant on the penultimate day of my End to End where it popped up on the side of the road. I like to salute unusual plants as I travel through the landscape, take a selfie with a particularly striking patch, make a note of something about the plant I've not noticed before.

Treasure in the field

On my last day of walking, only a couple of miles from John o'Groats, I turned up the next straight road to Stemster and surprised a doe at the edge of a barley field. It bounded away over the field, leaping high above the height of the ripening cereal and disappeared into a corner of the field with just its ears sticking up above the barley. I was completely amazed.

How much for this field?
Pure gold as it stretches ahead of me;
I'd give anything for this field.

To have that leaping doe on repeat,
bounding high over the barley.
I'd watch it all day, every day,
my cup overflowing.
How much for this field
burned now into my memory,
woven into my own cells,
a priceless treasure?

Activities for pilgrims in agricultural land

Look out for information about different farming practices, like organic farming.

Take time to walk a farm trail if possible.

Remember the country code: keep dogs on leads, close gates and do not drop litter.

Try to buy some local produce: eggs, honey or something else you can carry with you.

Visit an open farm if possible, or stay on a farm; support those who are trying to rewild the land.

Consider all aspects of a field: its edges, rows, gates, stiles, the sky above, the earth below. Respect the work of the agricultural community.

Stand in the landscape and feel the wind blow through.

Feel the soil with your fingers. Watch the smallest creatures toiling on the ground.

8. Geological landscapes

The Earth is ages old. Everywhere is a geological landscape but some places are particularly remembered or protected for specific features, a limestone pavement or chalk stream for example, a gorge or mountain. Some geological or geographical features may be named after a character in myth or legend, like the Giant's Causeway on the Antrim Coast (which was not on my End to End), or for a local saint, like St Ninian's Cave near Whithorn, which is named after the fourth-century hermit.

We can go back centuries but your story,
recalled in rocks and stones, is much older.
You speak to us through the stone.
Standing on the shore, close to Ninian's Cave,
the sea and land and sky combine
to tell a story of creative energy,
of renewal and hope:
we celebrate that hope.

On Windy Ridge

Some features receive local names that reveal something of the forces at work in the landscape. Windy by name is likely to mean windy by nature. Trees will grow in the direction of the prevailing wind.

I'm still standing,
though the weather does its best to flatten me.
Occasionally a route is named for a weather phenomenon,
a tribute to the generations who have recognised the challenge.

Remembering King Coal

God lifted me out of the horrible muddy pit and set my feet on rock, giving me a firm place to stand. (RB)

The extraction of fossil fuels has left marks on our global climate and on our landscapes. The route from Sanquhar to Cumnock in Upper Nithsdale, Dumfries and Galloway, is one where you will be able to see this for yourself in the humps and bumps of the landscape and the memorials to accidents above and below ground. You can learn more about a community – its stories, political struggles – in local institutes, miners' libraries and museums.

In Dumfries and Galloway it's interesting to the visit the Crawick Multiverse, where Charles Jencks has created a fantasy landscape inspired by space, astronomy and cosmology on the site of a huge former opencast coal mine. Various 'galaxies' have been created from the boulders found there – and when I visited in June 2019 the grounds were covered in wild orchids.

Compressed and fossilised,
excavated and exploited,
what now for King Coal?
The stuff that fuelled the world

now dishonoured and abandoned,
remembered only in the places scarred by its rise.
As the world turns
we turn old heaps into new enterprises
and generate our power on the breath of wind,
but below us and around us
the memories of King Coal still run deep.
God our rock, give us a firm place to stand.

Hills

The Unsleeping One keeps us company from the hills. (RB)

Even if you try to walk 'on the flat' by following canals and old railway lines, there will be hills. Some will be more challenging than others. The Lochaber Hills around Fort William and the west end of the Great Glen were used as a training ground for British forces during the Second World War. You can still see evidence of their training exercises on a marked route that also involves part of the Great Glen Way.

Some writers question whether or not long-distance walking routes like the West Highland Way or the Great Glen Way should be thought of as pilgrimages. Once again, I emphasise: it depends on the intentions of the pilgrim. Many of the more popular traditional pilgrim routes, like the Camino, have become quite busy and even congested by pilgrim-tourists in recent times. For my part I can still find the spiritual quality of pilgrimage on these long-distance trails. There are often local stories and half-forgotten places that can be reinstated into the pilgrim landscape. Furthermore, I'm no more able to look into the hearts of my fellow travellers than the next person, so I suggest it's best not to try to second-guess why anyone is going anywhere or under what motivation. Just keep journeying together.

The Great Glen is a major geological fault that crosses Scotland – and which provides some awesome scenery. It can also be quite wet. There's a small Hermit's Cave above Loch Ness which we have always enjoyed visiting. Only a very small hermit could live in it, much like the equally small cave in the Longdendale Valley in Derbyshire. Although St Benedict was once a hermit, it's not a calling he recommends in his Rule. Certainly these small caves would be uncomfortable for more than a fleeting visit. Even so, they are good places to pause and reflect.

There are many other caves of different sizes up and down Britain, opening up a whole underground world. Enter caves with caution, appropriate equipment and experienced guides.

When life goes underground,
and water makes a way
that opens up a new world,
admire the slow drip
that creates hidden beauty,
and tells us of the Timeless One
who also keeps watch from inside the hills.

Prayer in the old quarry

Since the Stone Age, humans have found rock to be quite useful in different ways. Our landscape still bears witness to this, from Neolithic monuments to stone quarries, some long-abandoned, others still working – and some developed into the next exciting tourist attraction with the addition of high-speed zip wires!

Near the reservoir called Bottoms in the Longdendale Valley is an old quarry that I often use as a cathedral. Slender trees meet overhead to form the vaulting. They sway in the breeze and, embroidered by the sounds of local birds – pigeons, crows, magpies and the occasional great spotted woodpecker – make a very comforting sound.

In a quarry near Tintwistle, a large flat rock forms an altar surrounded by a sea of heather, making a purple carpet in late summer.

Another one I enjoy visiting in the summer is near the Monsal Trail at Miller's Dale in Derbyshire. A disused limestone quarry, it is home to a wide array of limestone-loving plants and those that depend on them, like common blue butterflies.

God our rock,
may our worship be as wonderful
as the ageless hills
and the countless species
that praise you here.
May we serve you readily
in your roofless world,
open to every possibility,
and may we rest in your endless love
until your kindom comes.

Activities for pilgrims in geological landscapes

Rock may look tough but this may be an illusion. What signs of change do you see in the geological landscape you are visiting? A landslip or shapes indicating signs of erosion? You may see layers in exposed rock indicating previous ages of the Earth. The parallel roads of Glen Roy are not roads at all but the marks of shorelines of frozen lakes that melted after the last Ice Age.

Admire the rocks, their shapes and textures. You may even find fossils.

Find out what grows around rocky ground, between rocks, in gorges: even here there will be something clinging on.

Try out the echo in a rocky place.

Explore safely.

9. Industrial landscapes

Industrial or post-industrial landscapes are not necessarily places for pilgrims to avoid. Many now have official paths and greenways that go around or through them, like at the Sankey Canal in Warrington. Others will be the site of particular events, a mining accident, a Trade Union protest, a place of invention; all these can be places of pilgrimage.

The green corridor

Walking through the green, on a reused way,
I see the land has come to life again!
For the diversity of creation
from the tiny scarlet pimpernel flower
to the giant oak, sycamore and beech,
from the ladybird
to the grey heron:
All is wonderful.

For the support of friends and colleagues,
for shared visions and a shared journey,
for companions on the way:
All is wonderful.

Reusing old railway routes

God, show me the right path; point out the route I should follow. (RB)

The railways made a huge difference to Britain as their tracks criss-crossed the landscape, taking people and goods from place to place. They still do, but in addition disused railways have become a feature as walking routes.

Walking down the line,
straight enough with gentle gradient,
remembering times past
and the whiff of steam.

These routes are good for pilgrims of diverse abilities. I use these accessible, traffic-free routes as often as I can, as they are quieter, like green corridors.

The Trans Pennine Trail (TPT) makes use of the old Sheffield to Manchester line through the Longdendale Valley, and again from Dunford Bridge to the town of Penistone. Further east, the old route of the Hull to Hornsea Line provides the path. In other parts of Derbyshire, the county where I now live, there are routes like the High Peak Trail, the Tissington Trail and the Manifold Way. I've also walked from Beverley to Bubwith in East Yorkshire on disused railway routes. There are more than 8000 miles of disused railway lines across Britain, many open as accessible routes, enough to choose from for a day's journey or for a week or more. In 2022 my husband and I made a journey of several weeks from the south of the UK back to the north on the route of the former Great Central Railway, piecing together the disused, dismantled or disappeared line. You'll find guidebooks for the most accessible lines, which are promoted by the charity Sustrans.

How good it is, how pleasant,
that this path is still being used
as a sustainable traffic-free route.
Many old routes are reusable:
the country criss-crossed with paths used by our forebears.
We walk in the footsteps of those who have gone ahead of us,
and rejoice.

God of steam and diesel,
with lines now empty and stations abandoned,
we rejoice at the new ways,
the routes that have replaced the once-busy lines.
As we travel through the land,
may these green ways
be a sign of our commitment
to greener ways.

Of course a pilgrimage may also be made by rail. My father first went to Cornwall in 1939 as an evacuee, taking a train with his younger brother from Tottenham in North London to the village of Troon, near Camborne. He and his brother were cared for by a kind family, whom we visited many times in my childhood and with whom we remain in contact. My father's return pilgrimage to Cornwall in 2019 was, like his original journey as a nine-year-old boy, by rail.

As the signals stop and go,
and the trains arrive and depart,
when you come to the end of the track,
may the lifelong friends you have made
always welcome you back.

In the news

Sometimes a place where I have walked comes up in the national news. It was like that in early December 2020 when, in the midst of the Covid-19 pandemic, there was an explosion at a water treatment works at Avon-mouth. I'd walked past it in April 2019, and so quickly felt a connection to the people in that place when I heard it mentioned again.

Looking back, over my shoulder, I can see the ripped metal.
The shock waves are still reverberating
through the lives of the families caught up in the tragedy.
May we who walk past do so with the fullest heart,
for when this has all been repaired, the scars will remain:
our prayers will be needed long into the future,
and our willingness to make safer communities must be a high priority.

The Road to Wigan Pier

I read this book, by George Orwell, as a teenager for my O-Level English Literature, at the time understanding very little of it. These days Wigan Pier is a pub, a nearby mill is now an office, and other old industrial land has been converted to car parks. The canal still winds through the townscape.

We sat down by the water and remembered a better time and place.
In our exile how will we sing a happy song in this strange land? (RB)

The exiles are expected to sing happy songs in the place of their captivity.
They remember the songs but don't have the heart for them.
We do not always feel like singing happy songs.
As the years go by, the divisions in our society seem to be as deep as ever:
Children grow up in poverty,
more families rely on foodbanks.
I cannot sing happy songs about these things.
Christ of the five thousand fed, have mercy.
Grant us justice for all, and enough left over to dispel our deepest fears.

A derelict factory

When a factory is closed, or a mine building, sometimes different parts are taken down and reused elsewhere, like in a heritage trail or at the entrance to the town to honour past lives. But often the building is just abandoned to decay over time, its silhouette left as a sign of times passed.

As a site decays, cracks appear and wildlife often takes over. There is a network of small airfields across Britain, many used during wartime and then closed. I walked past one at Tain and another on the TPT in East Yorkshire:

Cracking up, after all this time,
new life pushing through, making different patterns.
Some resilient plants have chosen this place
and some creatures have joined them:
It's a new community.
When the cracks show in our communities,
may we have the courage to break out
and do your kindom-building in new ways.

Joining up the dots

Maybe a walk you've done many times or your current route intersects
with a route you've previously used. As a family we call this type of walk
'joining up the dots', and it was our main way of walking in 2021 as the
restrictions concerning Covid-19 eased. We have joined up various routes
up and down and across Britain. This allows for new connections, for
seeing things in a new way.

We are always going over old ground,
re-running things in our heads
that we said or did in different circumstances.
Ground us in the present, Walking One,
and may we lope along with you,
taking each day as your gift to us.

Activities for pilgrims in industrial landscapes

The ways in which industry has changed our landscape may be recent or historical. Consider how the impact of industry has altered the landscape you are visiting.

There are often information boards about disused routes and buildings; see what you can find out.

See how many species reclaiming an old industrial site you can find and identify: on the walls, on the ground, between the cracks …

Imagine the lives of those who previously occupied these places. What could the places be used for now?

Explore carefully and heed warning signs.

10. Urban areas

There is a river and its streams make God's city a glad place,
the holy place where God is living.

God is right there in the centre of that place and shall not be removed
but shall come to help that city all of the time. (RB)

There's so much to explore in urban areas: housing, high streets, retail
parks, shops, museums, cafés, industry … Walking round Stockport, for
example, you might follow a trail of giant frogs, each one named for a particular local concern and sponsored by a community group or business.

Begin your pilgrimage by thinking about some of the things you expect to see. This might depend on whether you are visiting an area for the first time or have been there before and have become familiar with the place.

Severn Beach is a small community outside Bristol that has been popular with holidaymakers in the past. A town trail provides landmarks to demonstrate what has changed for the 21st-century visitor. In 2012, when my daughter Hannah was walking her End to End, we visited Shirley's Café there at the end of the road by the Severn Way. When I walked through in 2019, the café was still there, still open, although Shirley had died; it was now run by her family members.

Menus may change but the welcome is the same.
A new generation takes over the running,
but the original principles of hospitality remain.

God is my high tower. (RB)

There are many kinds of high towers in the urban landscape: cooling towers, chimney stacks, high-rise blocks of flats. In Celtic times, tall round towers were used for defence. They therefore crop up in Celtic spirituality as an image of the strong presence of God, as defender and refuge. But not all towers turn out to be a refuge, as the residents of Grenfell Tower, in London, tragically found out on 14th June, 2017, when seventy-two people were killed in a fire there.

From way up here, we can see so much,
but other things remain hidden from view.
The concealed decisions of constructors
may only come to light when tragedy strikes.
God of the High Tower,

may our buildings reflect our honesty
and be made of integrity and justice.

There is a memorial to those who died in the Grenfell Tower fire at the foot of the building. So too, a memorial wall on the South Bank of the River Thames provides one space for remembering those who died in the UK during the Covid-19 pandemic. There are many kinds of urban memorials. Some last for centuries and others have only a fleeting presence. A decaying bunch of flowers on a bridge may indicate where someone lost their life. The pilgrim may pass other urban memorials or newsworthy places, like the site of the Peterloo Massacre in Manchester, or the Bristol docks, which are remembered for their part in the transatlantic slave trade.

There's no right way to greet such places. Some pilgrims may take a symbolic item and place it at a particular place, write on a heart or leave flowers. One timeless response is silence.

Be still, and know that I am God. (RB)

The Weaver's Cottage, Kilbarchan

Local conditions dictated the development of past industries. Placement depended on the availability of natural resources, connections for transporting goods and a workforce. Fast forward to the future and we find some of the remnants of those industries, for tourists to visit and reflect on, like the Weaver's Cottage at Kilbarchan.

'And why get anxious about what you wear? See how the wild flowers grow, without weaving or spinning. But not even King Solomon when he was showing off was dressed as well as one of these plants.' (RB)

Most of us no longer make our clothing from scratch. It's usually readily available, cheap enough and can be discarded just as quickly. We behave like King Solomon, without thought for the origins of what we wear or who made it, anxious only about what we look like. We need to give more thought to the just production of what we wear and what to do with the clothing we no longer need or want.

The Framework Knitters Museum at Ruddington, Nottinghamshire, has been restored to remind the visitor of the working and living conditions of the past. The small courtyard there was once home to several families and the knitting frames still in situ give an indication of the working conditions. Visiting the museum I was once again left asking why we give so little value to those who clothe us.

Here history and memory are woven together;
it's interesting how textiles and radical politics made this warp and weft.
The cry for justice by textile workers continues around the globe:
the struggle is not yet over.
Give a thought to what you wear!

Small stations

Where time moves on the fastest, other things may be left behind, like small train stations no longer serving a large population. These may provide a starting off point for a pilgrim or an end point where an infrequent service can round off the day. The Far North Line is like this and still links very small communities in the Far North of Scotland. At one of the stations, Rogart, the station buildings and siding are used to house pleasant accommodation, including old railway rolling stock remade for self-catering.

Rest here, wait.
The timetable still runs,
if less frequently.
Rest here, wait.
In the time between trains
there's time to dream,
remember and pray.

Monster main street

Other small places invent their own industry. As we noted on previous
visits to Drumnadrochit on the Great Glen Way, it's a thriving place –
thanks to the various sightings of the famed Loch Ness Monster and its
associated celebrity industry, dating back to St Columba. Most of the busi-
nesses on the main street, whether museums or shops or cafés, claim a
monster relationship of some kind. There are many depictions of Nessie,
but green and fluffy seems the most popular on the main street of Drumnadrochit. Less than practical in a cold loch, but perhaps providing a creative place to begin to reinvent our high streets.

If you want a monster bargain
get down to a monster shop.
May the places that rely on monster stories
know joy and delight in storytelling.

The overall message for the pilgrim is that God loves urban places as much
as rural ones. Take time to consider the ambience of town and city. Beside
an old dock in Hull there's a memorial to merchant seamen, telling the
stories of those lost at sea: they are not forgotten. On a bridge in the same

city there's a memorial that uses two overlapping circles to honour the mathematician, philosopher and priest John Venn. It's a representation of his eponymous diagram. A less obvious memorial in the pavement nearby recalls Ottobah Cugoano, a fifteen-year-old slave, freed in 1772.

Every city has a long and complex history of overlapping lives. Bridges, docks, factories, houses, the constant redevelopment of our urban places attest to a creativity that is constantly working with God's vision for a just and sustainable kindom. Nothing is unchangeable and everything is open to question and interpretation. Look out for such signs on your journeys.

God loves cities.
God wants them to thrive and be places of abundant life.
May the city constantly remember God
and, directed in God's ways,
be a fruitful place for all people.

Activities for pilgrims in urban areas

How does walking through a town or city make you feel? After a long walk through countryside on the Greenwich Meridian Trail, emerging at Canary Wharf in London felt very different. Surrounded by large buildings, glass reflecting light and heat, I wondered what it costs to maintain these huge power towers. What do you notice about the town or city as you travel through?

Enjoy the hospitality of a local place: a café, pub or shop, museum or other attraction, even for a short time.

Find out if there's a town trail, or look out for any information which may remember former residents, like the Blue Plaque scheme, or perhaps a stone placed in the pavement.

Some post boxes may be decorated to celebrate successful athletes: look out for these. What else could you celebrate with street furniture and how? Enjoy some yarn-bombing when you get home.

Watch from a bench or seat as people come and go.

Visit a local charity- or second-hand shop for something reusable you can take with you.

Pause for a moment of respect at any local memorial.

Talk to local people. Listen. Try to do so as deeply as possible. Add any observations to your thoughts and prayers for the people and the place.

11. Gardens and allotments

Access to the outdoors or to a garden or allotment was never more important than during the Covid-19 pandemic, when people were isolating. A
garden is not a given for the whole population of Britain. A window box
or plant pot may be the only tiny oasis available to some, and a public space
their essential breathing place.

Creator of all, as the garden continually changes,
so the new life emerging truly amazes me.
May we use the knowledge we have

to make the balanced decisions the world needs to thrive.
May we be responsible gardeners and may the earth be renewed.

I love gardens and during my travels I often visit well-known larger ones.
I'd always wanted to visit the Eden Project in Cornwall, a thoughtful reuse
of an old industrial landscape. There is a small labyrinth at Eden, and there
are many others scattered across Britain. Of course you could make your
own on a shore or moor, in a churchyard or field or garden. I used to use
a lot of scarves and lengths of fabric to mark out the lines when I did this
as a school chaplain in Yorkshire, but stones, shells, twigs, or even rubbish
could be used to make a thoughtful route.

A garden path can be a labyrinth:
gentling walk into calm centre,
letting go and welcoming peace.

A garden path can be a launch pad:
revving up and counting down,
preparing me to face the world.

Look carefully and you can find wildlife in most places. I find snails almost
everywhere, like clinging to the surface of my door or windowsill. Wait
quietly and watch for wildlife in allotments, at bird tables in gardens and
bird feeders on balconies. Woodlice are also frequent visitors in my garden.
They may be very small creatures but they all count.

A fox in an allotment,
a rat in the bins,
bats in the belfry
and hedgehogs in the gutter:
wildlife is all around us

if we watch and listen.
Only a shared world is a thriving world.

At this table, the birds gather.
A mixed crowd, they squabble and squawk;
a few feathers fly.
Eventually they fly off to return tomorrow.
Sound familiar?

The Potter's house

In the Great Glen Way, a long trail across the middle of the Scottish Highlands, there is a potter's house with a beautiful wild garden.

God said, 'Go down to the potter's house, and there I will give you my message.' So I went down to the potter's house. (RB)

A lot of images in the Bible are taken from daily life. In this one Jeremiah sees the potter reshaping the wonky clay and it reminds him that God can reshape us, but only if we are willing to let God work on us. A walk is full of promising images: fungi spring up everywhere and ants scurry about working together. It depends on how we read the world around us and our relationship with it. We can be remade on any route, if we adopt that purpose.

In your hands, Creative Potter, reshape us
and fit us for your world to thrive alongside the fungi and the ants.

Heatwave

During a heatwave in July 2022, when several UK temperature records were broken, the conflict between climate change and our human habits became acute. Several houses were burnt down when wildfires from local grasslands or gardens got out of control. Families were left homeless. We began to see that high temperatures were not just an opportunity for a nice day at the beach but might have a significant impact on our homes, travel and work life. Walking in a heatwave is about more than just making sure you have enough water or shady places to rest. We each have responsibilities: climate change is real and is happening now.

Burnt grass, smoke rising, the pungent smell on the wind.
Help us to acknowledge our own part in such unwelcome effects;
how can we change, how can we speak up,
what must be our next step?

Hand in hand with our neighbours, from north and south, east and west,
may we take the action needed to restore
the fragile balance of our planet.

Activities for pilgrims visiting gardens

A garden may be the simplest place for a pilgrimage. Even a small garden presents many opportunities to notice and reflect and to create a green space to share with other species.

Visit a labyrinth, and maybe even make one yourself.

Set up a feeding station for hedgehogs or a bird table and wait and see who comes to the feast (remember to keep these clean as viruses can pass between creatures that use such stations).

Plant friendly gardens with species for insects of all kinds. Remember that many of these have life stages that require different plants or refuges. A nettle or bramble patch will not be wasted.

Make a small pond, or a wet area in a bucket or sink, or just set out a bowl of pebbles. It's even possible for a duck to nest on a high-rise balcony.

A bug hotel may be made from a pile of sticks or leftover pieces of wood, twigs and leaves.

12. Churchyards

And they crucified him. (RB)

There was one very consistent observation the length of Britain: the cross. From Land's End to John o'Groats, crosses of different ages pepper the land-scape. This Christian sign has been present here more or less since the

Roman occupation.

At Land's End the first village is Sennen, where the church was founded in 520 AD. That's before Columba landed on Iona (563 AD) or Augustine made it to Kent (597 AD). There are a number of early Christian slab crosses in the churchyard. There were several others on my first day's walk to Lamorna. This part of West Cornwall is known as a land of the early saints, often from the West of Ireland en route to Brittany. This probably accounts for the early foundation at Sennen.

Cross standing,
Cross waiting,
Cross telling
the old story.

For over 1500 years, crosses would be erected on buildings of worship or in the public square. They would be used to preach the gospel or to remember the dead, particularly during and after the two world wars of the 20th century. Each community had its own monument.

Cross standing,
Cross waiting,
Cross remembering
name after name.

The Far North also had its many crosses, including the rectangular Pictish cross slabs, like the one in Nigg Old Church dating from the eighth century. Now standing inside the church, it is said to show the earliest representation of the Eucharist in Christian art in Britain.

Cross standing,
Cross waiting,

Cross feeding
gathering community.

One of the most elaborate crosses in Scotland – decorated with scenes from the life of Christ – is the Ruthwell Cross in Dumfries and Galloway. This cross was erected, then pulled down, and finally restored.

Here it stands, after all this time,
silently telling the story,
and central to it all,
carved in stone and irrefutable:
He was crucified.

When I survey this wondrous cross …

A Saxon cross dating from the seventh century can be found in the parish church at Nunburnholme near Pocklington on the Pilgrimage of Grace Trail. Sections of the broken cross were found walled up in the church and then reconstructed and resurrected in the nave. The carving, showing the steps of the Christian story from the Incarnation to glory, is basic, early Christian in style, reminding us of just how old the cross-story is in our land.

Shall I mention your name, shall I?
Do I need to say it here?
Shall I whisper or speak it aloud?
It's all here, the story in stone:
a mother and child,
some episodes of adult life,
a criminal's death.
Where's the glory in that?

Those who look for different gods
may have forgotten your name
but I speak it aloud: Jesus!

Launceston, the border town of Cornwall, has a medieval preaching cross
in the churchyard, which I didn't expect to see there:

The sun, dancing,
lights up all the lanes,
from Land's End to Launceston,
where I step out and meet you –
an unexpected surprise,
so gently encouraging.

Launceston's church is dedicated to St Mary Magdalene and is remembered
in a poem by local writer Charles Causley. There is a reclining statue of the
saint carved into an outside end wall of the church. A local custom says
that if you can land a stone on this statue, you will be rewarded with a new
set of clothes.

Are you resting, Mary?
I'm surprised.
Isn't there much to do
to tell the gospel here?
Are you resting, Mary?
Or encouraging visitors
to land a stone
and hear a story?

The most common patron saint of Church of England churches is St Mary
the Virgin. Less common local patron saints may also be encountered, like

Arilda, a fifth- or sixth-century female saint from the Oldbury area of Gloucestershire. One of the two churches dedicated to her is there, on the site of an Iron Age hillfort, and St Arilda's Well is not far away.

A name, a stone, a story:
the landscape reveals the lost ones.
Admire the view by all means
but do not neglect the new life
bubbling up at your feet.

One of the most often used and best-remembered parts of the Bible in relation to the story of Mary, the mother of Jesus, is the Magnificat. I often sing a version of it when pilgrimaging or make up a new version using my remembered Bible. Here's a reminder of the Magnificat, Mary's Song:

Come let us make God bigger, as Mary did.
Let us rejoice in knowing God, as Mary did.
Like Mary, we are not important in the universe.
Even so, God has blessed us, as Mary was blessed.
Through us God's ways may be known in the world,
just as Mary made them known, lifting up the poor and humble,
putting down arrogant ones, sending the rich away empty.
For we are part of the human family stretching back to Abraham and Sarah,
through whom God has promised many things, just as Mary was.
And so we too give glory to God, Creator, Son and Holy Spirit, as Mary did.

The comedian Frankie Howerd is buried in the churchyard of St Gregory at Weare. We were eating our picnic lunch on a bench here when a local person asked if we were looking for him. Like Mary Magdalene, I was looking for the gardener.

We shall be changed,
from down-to-earth comedian
to something else.
When the locals ask 'Who is it you're looking for?'
What is your reply?

'To church via radical steps' is a notice in Kirkby Lonsdale, Cumbria.

There are 86 'radical steps' in a flight up to the church from the River Lune. The concept of 'radical steps' appealed to me.

There are many ways of thinking about radical steps. In some ways the fifty-seven days it had taken me to walk the five hundred miles to get here were radical steps, as that's not such a common activity in Britain these days. Fewer people walk long distances than in previous generations as it's no longer as necessary. We may discover it's good for us but it's still a minority activity.

Of course there are other ways to think about radical steps, including stepping out for change in attitudes and activities, for example in response to climate change and ecological threats. Many in the past have taken radical steps together, for example the Jarrow Marchers (1936). You can probably think of others. The why, how and where of marches like this, the radical steps they entail, are still a relevant form of non-violent protest.

Add my radical steps to yours, Companion Christ.

Reused churches

Jesus said to Zaccheus, 'I'm coming to your house for tea!' (RB)

Reusing churches as cafés or restaurants is a reasonably common find in both urban and rural areas. The dwindling of congregations has led to churches closing across Britain, and to opportunities for their creative reuse. I had soup in one at Gourock and cake in another at Ewich on the West Highland Way. The old tin chapel at Kinbrace is now reused as a community hall. It's possible to stay the night in some disused churches: this is called 'champing'. Many churchyards are now part of rewilding projects, providing bird and bat boxes, hives and bee hotels.

When the door is shut for the last time,
is the table really empty?

A church that serves tea and cake is following in a Jesus tradition, although I've yet to see one called Chez Zaccheus. In some I found a welcome laid out in style: water, a kettle, nice biscuits … It was a help-yourself honesty system, but unfortunately many churches had to close during 2020 due to the pandemic, so I don't know how much of this service of refreshment will have survived.

At Zach's house you sat down to eat,
causing a stir in more than a teacup.
We, who struggle to invite more than our friends,
need you to change us from lukewarm hosts
to radical feast-sharers.
Please sit down with us.

Prayer at a well

Before churches were built, wells were often the gathering point for a local community. They remind us of a time when domestic water didn't come from taps, and wells were essential and visited daily. Wells are often connected with local legends, which were appropriated by Christians to tell another story. Some wells gained reputations as holy places of healing. I try to pause at a well, and if it is still possible, touch the water that is there.

Water is life and life-giving water a valuable gift.
We pray for all those who wait for water,
who live in need of adequate water supplies;
and for those who have the engineering skill
to bring water to where it is needed.
May the resources for life be shared fairly.

St Trostan's Cemetery, Caithness

In the Far North, on a blustery day, I visited this old cemetery near Thurso. There's a water stoup in the wall here that may be medieval in origin and possibly from the church of St Trostan, who may have been called Drostan, who may have come from Ireland. Such are the layers of stories in the landscape.

Storytelling One, you know how it goes,
each layer built on another,
first passed on by word of mouth.
As we touch the water,
remind us of our promise
to live wet, whatever the weather,
and rise again with you,
released, changed, remade
by our shared adventures.

Activities for pilgrims visiting churchyards

Think about these words, carved on the stone labyrinth at Dalswinton:

Look where you have been,
view where you are at,
seek where you want to be

Churchyards are often havens for wildlife. What wildlife, or evidence of wildlife, can you spot? Birds, rabbits, foxes, badgers ... ? How is the church you're visiting addressing the issues of rewilding and climate change? The churchyard may be under the care of God's Acre, a project that works with local churches to encourage wildlife.

The gravestones and memorials will give you some idea of the history of the area. Dates on the stones will indicate how long the churchyard has been in use. Some will be carved with leaves and flowers, skulls and other memento mori; some may say the type of work people did. Look around and see what you can find.

If you find a well or water stoup that is easily accessible and has water, dip your finger in and make the sign of the cross on your forehead or chest or hand. Listen to water flowing, or ask a companion to describe the sound to you. We all use our senses differently. A deaf or visually impaired person could also describe the experience to a hearing or sighted companion.

On a day when there is dew on the grass, take off your shoes and socks and feel the damp grass on your feet.

If there's a cross, sit by it and remember, alone or with others, the story of the Cross-Wise One. What do you recall? How do you retell it? How do you name Jesus?

Bibliography

Celtic Crosses of Britain and Ireland, M. Seaborne, Shire Archaeology, 1989

Lost Railway Walks, J. Holland, Harper Collins, 2019

Mazes and Labyrinths in Great Britain, J. Martineau, Wooden Books Ltd, 2005

Saints and Holy Places of Yorkshire: A Pilgrim's Guide to God's Own County, G. Wakefield, Sacristy Press, 2020

The Lost Rainforests of Britain, G. Shrubsole, Harper Collins, 2022

The Meaning of Geese: A Thousand Miles in Search of Home, N. Acheson, Chelsea Green, 2023

The Saints of Cornwall: 1500 Years of Christian Landscape, C.R. John, Tabb House, 2001

The Way Under Our Feet, G.B. Usher, SPCK, 2020

Wanderlust: A History of Walking, R. Solnit, Verso, 2001

Resources

British Pilgrimage Trust:
https://britishpilgrimage.org

Butterfly Conservation Trust:
https://butterfly-conservation.org

Canal and River Trust:
https://canalrivertrust.org.uk

Caring for God's Acre:
www.caringforgodsacre.org.uk

Champing, camping in churches:
https://champing.co.uk

'Clothing Dinogad' or 'Dinogad's Smock':
https://esmeraldamac.wordpress.com/2012/01/03/dinogads-smock-a-6th-century-cumbrian-lullaby/
and sung at https://www.youtube.com/watch?v=LOHNu5V11bI

Crawick Multiverse:
www.crawickmultiverse.co.uk

Framework Knitters Museum at Ruddington, Nottinghamshire:
https://frameworkknittersmuseum.org.uk

Long Distance Walkers Association:
https://ldwa.org.uk

Lost Rainforests of England:
https://lostrainforestsofengland.org

National Biodiversity Network, State of Nature Report, 2023:
https://nbn.org.uk/news/state-of-nature-2023

Routes of LEJoG:
https://bobjanet.org.uk/pilgrimage/lejogroutes.html

Royal Society for Protection of Birds:
www.rspb.org.uk

Slimbridge and other Wildfowl and Wetlands Trust sites:
www.wwt.org.uk/wetland-centres

Slow Ways: Help Create a National Walking Network:
https://beta.slowways.org

Sustrans:
www.sustrans.org.uk

The Eden Project:
www.edenproject.com

The Wild Flower Society:
https://thewildflowersociety.org.uk

The Woodland Trust:
www.woodlandtrust.org.uk

Wildlife Trusts:
www.wildlifetrusts.org

Locations of photos

Cover (and others)
Walking towards Thurso, Caithness

Page 14
Land's End signpost, Cornwall

Page 22
An oak tree on the Severn Way near Tewkesbury, Gloucestershire

Page 24
Sue's Cake Shed near Bunloit on the Great Glen Way

Page 27
Wild strawberries near Cumnock

Page 40
John o'Groats trail sign at John o'Groats

Page 47
St Michael's Mount, across Mount's Bay, Cornwall

Page 53
Beach path near Dunrobin Castle

Page 55
View from near Kingshouse on the West Highland Way

Page 57
The Lairig Mor on the West Highland Way

Page 61
Looking towards Fort William from the West Highland Way

Page 63
Canal tunnel entrance at Preston Brook, Cheshire

Page 69
Ox-eye daisies near Dunnet Bay, Caithness

Page 71
Road from Lothbeg, Sutherland

Page 72
Ferry Wood, Loch Fleet Nature Reserve, near Golspie, Sutherland

Page 78
Greylag geese at RSPB Frampton Marshes, Lincolnshire

Page 83
Swan and cygnets on the Shropshire Union Canal

Page 87
Holt Fleet bridge on the Severn Way

Page 89
Stepping stones towards Kinlochleven on the West Highland Way

Page 90
Cauliflower growing near Praze-an-Beeble, Cornwall

Page 91
Gateway near Locharbriggs, Dumfries and Galloway

Page 95
Barley field near Clifton Dykes, Cumbria

Page 97
Outside St Ninian's Cave, Whithorn, Dumfries and Galloway

Page 99
At Crawick Multiverse

Index of places